The Thin Tweed Line

Works by Jack Simmons
Published by SwanHorse Press

A Tropical Affair

The Thin Tweed Line

Three Dashes Bitters

The Thin Tweed Line

A Metaphysical Comedy

Jack Simmons

This is a work of fiction. Names, characters, places, and incidents portrayed in this play either are the product of the author's imagination or are used fictitiously. Any resemblance to actual persons, living or dead, events, or locales is entirely coincidental.

THE THIN TWEED LINE

A SwanHorse Press Book

Copyright © 2022, 2024 by Jack Simmons

All rights reserved

"Wooden background with American flag" vector by Freepik
"Seamless tweed fabric texture" by magann on CrushPixel

No part of this book may be reproduced, stored in a retrieval system, or transmitted by any means, electronic, mechanical, photocopying, recording, or otherwise, without written permission from the publisher or author, except in the case of brief quotations embodied in critical articles or reviews.

All inquiries regarding professional or amateur performance rights should be addressed to Monte Ceceri Publishers.

Simmons, Jack, 1964– author
The thin tweed line: A play in three acts / Jack Simmons
ISBN: 978-1-949512-05-2 (KDP paperback)
ISBN: 978-1-949512-17-5 (IS paperback)
ISBN: 978-1-949512-19-9 (eBook)
1. Drama — Philosophy. 2. American drama.
3. Comedy. 4. Satirical plays. 5. American wit and humor.
6. Love stories, American. 7. United States — Fiction. I. Title

Monte Ceceri Publishers
P.O. Box 60623
Savannah, GA 31420
www.montececeri.com

The Thin Tweed Line premiered in Savannah, Georgia, at the Jenkins Hall Black Box Theater, April 28–May 1, 2022.

STUDENTS

MARGOT	Ivy Robertson
TRACY	Kathryn Bauer
PROTESTERS	Carson Gray, Noslen German, Skyler Griffin, Vivian Elam

FACULTY

SARAH MORGAN	Ellie Strickland
STANLEY STEVENSON	Vuk Pavlovic
MILTON SAWYER	Minh Nguyen
HELEN MIRANDARI	Whitney Ketron

ADMINISTRATION

LINDA THOMPSON	Leigh E. Rich

DIRECTED BY	Jack Simmons
LIGHTING, SOUND, AND DESIGN	Katherine Simmons

The Thin Tweed Line

A Metaphysical Comedy

Jack Simmons

Characters

STUDENTS

MARGOT	A senior and a leader of the Conservative Christian Campus Crusade (CCCC)
TRACY	A new student, also with the CCCC
CONSERVATIVE PROTESTERS	Other members of the CCCC
FEMINIST PROTESTERS	Members of the Campus Feminists

FACULTY

SARAH MORGAN	Associate Professor of Philosophy as well as Gender and Women's Studies
STANLEY STEVENSON	Professor of Philosophy
MILTON SAWYER	Professor of Philosophy and Economics
HELEN MIRANDARI	Professor of Gender and Women's Studies and Business; Arlington Award Scholar

ADMINISTRATION

LINDA THOMPSON	Dean of the College of Liberal Arts

Setting

The campus of a small liberal arts university in the South. Modern day.

Act I

Scene 1

Clad in a tweed suit, STANLEY sits outside at a table reading a book. Behind him a sign says "Tobacco-Free Campus." Drinking from a coffee cup, he takes a sip, then dumps the coffee into a planter next to him. He draws a small flask from his jacket and pours its contents into the cup. A group of FEMINIST PROTESTERS — with signs that include "Safe Spaces," "The Future is Female," and "Deconstruct Privilege" — march past. STANLEY ignores them. The PROTESTERS stop in front of STANLEY and chant, "Death to the patriarchy! Death to the patriarchy!" Head still in book, he gives them a thumbs up. The PROTESTERS move on, still chanting, and STANLEY finally looks up to see if they have gone. He shudders, downs the remainder of his drink in a single gulp, and closes his book. He stands up and walks off in the opposite direction.

Scene 2

MARGOT enters and sits at the table STANLEY just vacated. She waits impatiently, looking at her phone. TRACY enters and joins MARGOT.

MARGOT: Where have you been?

TRACY: Sorry, class went over.

MARGOT: Ugh, I hate it when professors won't stop teaching. Like I don't have anything better to do.

TRACY: I don't mind. I like the subject.

MARGOT: There's a cute boy in the class?

TRACY: I wish.

MARGOT: This place is a desert.

TRACY: I haven't met anyone I liked.

MARGOT: You have standards?

TRACY: Well, I like boys who are…

MARGOT: What?

TRACY: Smart.

MARGOT: Good luck.

TRACY: But this is a university.

FEMINIST PROTESTERS enter and march across the stage — repeatedly chanting, "Deconstruct male privilege!" — and then exit.

MARGOT: It's a numbers game. Seventy-five percent of the students are women.

TRACY: The odds —

MARGOT: Are against you. Three girls for every boy. And you want a smart one.

TRACY: Yes, so —

MARGOT: So you've met the men who attend this university. How many are smart?

TRACY: Um —

> FEMINIST PROTESTERS *shout from offstage: "Girls rule, boys drool!"*

MARGOT: Exactly. There aren't many. There are so many girls, the smart boys get snapped up like lifeboats on the *Titanic*.

TRACY: I didn't think of it that way.

MARGOT: College isn't what it used to be. When my mom attended this university, there were five men for every woman. She had her pick. It was like Disneyland for women.

TRACY: What happened?

> *Shouting from offstage: "Death to the patriarchy!"*

MARGOT: I don't think they feel safe.

TRACY: I didn't realize that the university would be —

> FEMINIST PROTESTERS *enter again and march across the stage.* MARGOT *pulls out her phone to film them.*

PROTESTER LEADER: What do we want?

PROTESTER ONE: A rejection of essentialist ideologies and the phallic economy!

PROTESTER LEADER: When do we want it?

PROTESTER TWO: Now!

> FEMINIST PROTESTERS *repeat their chants until they exit.*

TRACY: — dominated by women.

MARGOT: Welcome to the twenty-first century.

TRACY: Who are these women?

MARGOT: Postmodern feminists.

TRACY: I don't understand.

MARGOT: Postmodernists have been beguiled by the notion that all their problems are someone else's fault.

Shouting from offstage: "The patriarchy is killing us!"

TRACY: Men?

MARGOT: Mostly. And women like us.

TRACY: We aren't part of the patriarchy.

MARGOT: They would disagree.

Shouting from offstage, in a call-and-response format and repeated twice: "What do we want?"... "Safe spaces for women!"

TRACY: What is a "safe space"?

MARGOT: A place where there are no men.

TRACY: Like this campus?

MARGOT: Exactly.

Shouting from offstage: "If you aren't angry, you aren't paying attention!"

MARGOT: They believe that women can't be happy because they are oppressed by men. If you are happy, it is because you are participating in male privilege.

TRACY: Participating in the patriarchy?

MARGOT: Aligned with masculine interests rather than feminine interests.

TRACY: How?

MARGOT: You want to meet a man, right?

TRACY: Yes.

MARGOT: Get married?

TRACY: Of course.

MARGOT: Have his children?

TRACY: Sure.

MARGOT: And there it is. You, Tracy, have aligned your interest with the interests of men. Your happiness hinges upon masculine power, which means you're part of the patriarchy.

TRACY: And therefore —

MARGOT: You are supporting the oppression of women, so you do not count as a real woman. You're a traitor to your gender.

TRACY: So...to be a real woman means being angry.

MARGOT: That's postmodern feminism.

TRACY: But I'm not angry. A little frustrated, perhaps, but not angry.

Shouting from offstage: "If you aren't angry, you are part of the problem!"

MARGOT: You're either with them or against them.

TRACY: Well, I guess I am with them.

MARGOT: Are you sure?

TRACY: I'm a feminist.

Shouting from offstage: "Death to toxic masculinity!"

TRACY: What is "toxic masculinity"?

MARGOT: Men.

Shouting from offstage: "You're either with us or against us!"

TRACY (*loudly and to the* PROTESTERS *offstage*): Against!

MARGOT: They want men to change their behavior.

TRACY: How so?

MARGOT: To be more in touch with their feelings and comfortable expressing emotions.

TRACY: So it would be better if men were —

MARGOT: Like women.

TRACY: Making the campus —

MARGOT: An all-girls school.

Shouting from offstage: "The future is female!"

TRACY (*sarcastically*): Great. We wish there were more men around —

MARGOT: And they wish there weren't any.

Shout from offstage: "Death to the patriarchy and organized religion!"

MARGOT: It's not safe to be a Christian at this university.

TRACY: So we're both victims of the patriarchy?

MARGOT: No, we are Christians. We like the patriarchy.

Shouting from offstage: "Don't make deals with the patriarchy!"

MARGOT: We are oppressed by the postmodernists.

TRACY: So we are both oppressed?

MARGOT: No. Our oppression is the *real* oppression. This country is falling prey to the radical liberal agenda.

TRACY: What agenda?

MARGOT: They want America to be anti-Christian, anti-family, and anti-American. We are on the front lines of a holy war — a war for the soul of the nation.

TRACY: We are the front line?

MARGOT: Against these women. And the professors.

TRACY: The professors?

MARGOT: What do they do, apart from seduce their students and attempt to undermine conservative, Christian values? They are all in conspiracy against us.

TRACY (*intrigued*): They seduce students?

MARGOT: These professors, in their quaint tweed jackets with those gross elbow patches, lure you in with their *Beyond Good and Evil* philosophy.

TRACY: Which professors?

MARGOT: And what useful skills do they teach us — the metaphysical philosophy of Aristotle or the metaphysical poetry of John Donne?

TRACY: I like John Donne.

MARGOT: We pay a fortune in tuition — and for what? Diplomas that aren't worth the paper they are printed on.

TRACY: On which they are printed.

MARGOT: What?

TRACY: You ended the sentence with a preposition.

MARGOT: My point exactly. That is what I will learn from four years of college, not to end a sentence with a preposition. How will that help me find a job?

TRACY: I don't know.

MARGOT: If I give McDonald's five dollars, I get a happy meal. If I give Ford or Chevrolet thirty thousand dollars, I get a car. By the time I graduate, I will have given this university enough money for a small house. And what will I have? A mass of knowledge designed to undermine my values and make me unemployable.

Shouting from offstage: "The university doesn't educate us — it indoctrinates us!"

TRACY: Sounds the same as the feminists.

MARGOT: Not at all. You will see. You will be at *our* rally today, right?

TRACY: Of course. I have posters, flyers, buttons, bumper stickers, everything.

MARGOT: Good. I've got a megaphone and mace.

TRACY: Do you really think anyone will come?

MARGOT: There are thousands of students like us, afraid to speak their minds for fear of retaliation. It is up to us to change the campus climate and make it safe for conservative Christians again.

TRACY: I will be there, but... (*sheepishly*) I have a meeting with a professor now.

MARGOT: With who?

TRACY: Whom.

MARGOT: Whatever.

TRACY: I am going to see Professor Stevenson.

MARGOT: The philosophy professor?

TRACY: I know…he is kind of cute — in that sort of "old-man-in-a-tweed-jacket" way.

MARGOT: I think you mean "old-creeper-in-a-tweed-jacket" way.

TRACY (*incredulously, drawing out her name*): Margot.

MARGOT: He is a philosophy professor. They are the worst. You should record the conversation. For your protection.

TRACY: Protection from what?

MARGOT *grabs* TRACY's *phone and hits some buttons.*

MARGOT: Just press this while it's in your pocket, and you are recording. You can't be too careful, especially with the philosophers. Remember, record everything!

TRACY *nods, stands up, and begins to walk away.*

TRACY: See you at the rally!

MARGOT (*standing as well*): Remember, record everything!

Scene 3

LINDA *sits outside at a table drinking coffee.* FEMINIST PROTESTERS *march by demanding safe spaces for women, then exit.* SARAH *enters, carrying her own cup of coffee, and approaches* LINDA.

SARAH: Quite a rally, Linda.

LINDA: I organized it.

SARAH (*sitting down*): I know. I wanted —

LINDA: To thank me? I know, right? Women need this: a safe space on campus to discuss issues unique to their experiences. That is why we are organizing — to show broad support for women's issues and fight the oppression women face daily on this campus.

SARAH: Uh-huh, but I came to speak with you about my grant proposal —

LINDA's *cell phone rings.*

LINDA: Excuse me. (*Answering her phone.*) Dean Thompson speaking. (*Pause.*) Just a minute. (*To* SARAH.) What were you saying?

SARAH: My —

LINDA: Oh, yes, my safe spaces. Hold on.

SARAH: No, my —

LINDA (*holding her hand up to stop* SARAH *and speaking into the phone*): What? (*Pause.*) Yes. (*Pause.*) Yes, impressive rally, isn't it? (*Pause.*) Uh-huh. (*Pause.*) Why, thank you, we are trying to make this campus safe for women's voices. (*Disappointed.*) Oh damn — I mean, that's too bad. (*Pause.*) I am with Sarah now. (*Pause.*) Yes, Sarah Morgan, in the Philosophy Department. You know, I think she can help me...

LINDA *hangs up her phone and sets it on the table.*

SARAH: Help you with what?

LINDA: I need to find a date for Professor Helen Mirandari.

SARAH: Excuse me?

LINDA: That was Diana in Accounting. She failed.

SARAH: To find a date for Helen?

LINDA: Yes. And I was counting on her.

SARAH: Anyway, about my grant —

LINDA: You have met Helen, haven't you? Professor Helen Mirandari? Brilliant woman!

SARAH: Uh-huh.

LINDA: Our Arlington Award Scholar?

SARAH: Uh-huh.

LINDA: Uses gender theory to deconstruct economic theory.

SARAH: I know who she is.

LINDA: Then why are you so dubious?

SARAH: I don't doubt her existence, I doubt —

LINDA: Her scholarship?

SARAH: Your sanity.

LINDA: My sanity?

SARAH: I thought we were meeting to talk about my grant.

LINDA: Look, this is important. I convinced her to come here from Whitefield College.

SARAH: I know. Quite the coup, luring a high-powered scholar from an elite Northeastern college.

LINDA: The problem is she's unhappy.

SARAH: Unhappy? She has an endowed position and a joint appointment in Gender and Women's Studies and the Business School. She probably earns more money than all the faculty in my department combined. How can she be unhappy?

LINDA: Turns out that high-powered college in Upstate New York was so isolated, she couldn't meet any eligible men.

> She admitted to me that she only agreed to come here because she thought it would be easier to meet someone.

SARAH: Excuse me?

LINDA: I know, I know.

SARAH: The university's leading scholar in women's studies came here to find a man?

LINDA: Well, when you put it that way —

SARAH: What other way is there to put it? But as terrifying as that is, what I really can't understand is why you are involved. You are the dean —

LINDA: Yes.

SARAH: A dean's job now includes matchmaking?

LINDA: I am afraid that she will leave.

SARAH: Let her leave.

LINDA: I can't.

SARAH: Why not?

LINDA: I plan to leverage my success in recruiting her in my application for the new vice president of academic affairs position.

SARAH: The provost position?

LINDA: Yes!

SARAH: So your quest to find her a lifelong companion is —

LINDA: Thoughtful?

SARAH: Motivated by your own ambition.

LINDA: Oh. Well, after what I've done for this university, I deserve to be the provost.

SARAH: So why are you telling me all this?

LINDA: I need your help.

SARAH: Dating help?

LINDA: Yes.

SARAH: Tell her to try the Internet. Isn't that how people meet now?

LINDA: She said she tried but that all the men were either married or "creepy."

SARAH: Well yeah, it's the Internet. Isn't that the point?

LINDA: I suppose. The problem is she's thirty-nine, single, and wants a family. Like so many of us, she put her career first, and now she feels like she is running out of —

SARAH: Time.

LINDA: Yes.

SARAH: God, I pity women like you.

LINDA: It is hard to be a liberated, heterosexual woman.

SARAH: I wouldn't know.

LINDA: You have it so easy.

SARAH: Really?

LINDA: Men are impossible. I finally gave up. It was easier.

SARAH: You should tell Helen to give up. Men always disappoint.

LINDA: I did, but she has this absurd fantasy about Christmas morning and such.

SARAH: What?

LINDA: She isn't like us. She grew up in a family that likes one another. Her parents are still happily married. Her brothers return home for the holidays with their wives and children.

SARAH: That sounds horrible.

LINDA: Nevertheless, that is what she wants.

SARAH: So you need to find a man for the university's leading feminist scholar so she can get married, have kids, and satisfy her Christmas morning fantasy?

LINDA: Yes.

SARAH: And support the patriarchy through the celebration of another male savior.

LINDA: The irony is not lost on me.

SARAH: This is not ironic. It is tragic.

LINDA: Nevertheless —

SARAH: So what is the problem? There are plenty of men on campus.

LINDA: Are there? Really?

SARAH: More than half the faculty are —

LINDA: Idiots.

SARAH: I was going to say "men."

LINDA: Oh yes, but are they eligible?

SARAH: You mean Helen has standards?

LINDA: Oh no. Heavens no. She made it perfectly clear that she would date any man who didn't take up two seats on an airplane and who didn't support supply-side economics.

SARAH: So?

LINDA: So…think about the men you know on this campus.

SARAH: Yes.

LINDA: They are all married or gay.

SARAH (*thinking as she counts on her fingers*): Gosh, I hadn't considered it, but…(*laughing*) there are not many available men. What about Milton? He is a —

LINDA: Pig.

SARAH: Well —

LINDA: A pig in a cheap tweed suit with an affected accent.

SARAH: I was going to say "one of the college's great minds."

LINDA: He has slept with every available woman who works here and some who are not, strictly speaking, "available."

SARAH: I haven't slept with him.

LINDA: I hardly think that improves his candidacy.

SARAH: I don't know. Seems to me he is an ideal candidate.

LINDA: Ideal for what? To get her drunk, to seduce her with lies, to leave her alone, hungover, and smelling of cheap aftershave in a fleabag motel on the south side of town?

There is a long pause. SARAH *stares at* LINDA, *then at the audience, then back at* LINDA.

SARAH: And there is the not-so-small matter of his being married.

LINDA: Is he still married?

SARAH: It is, if I understand correctly, a marriage of convenience. I believe that they married in graduate school for the sake of citizenship.

LINDA: His or hers?

SARAH: Or was it tax evasion? I don't know, but I don't think Milton has spoken with her in years. Still, I suppose it disqualifies him from the Christmas morning fantasy.

LINDA: And then there is the issue of his computer hacking.

SARAH *laughs.*

LINDA: It isn't funny. Last week, he hacked into the university's server and uploaded a picture of Mussolini for my profile photo.

SARAH (*laughing*): I know, I saw it. Are you sure it's him?

LINDA: Yes, and when I can prove it, he will be fired.

SARAH: OK, so who do you have in mind?

LINDA: Stanley Stevenson.

SARAH *spits her coffee across the table.*

LINDA: What?

SARAH: You despise Stanley.

LINDA: He is everything that is wrong with this university. I know...but desperate times call for —

SARAH: Stanley?

LINDA: God, when you put it that way...but I suppose if he is dating Helen, he might lay off the coeds for a while.

SARAH: And what about my grant?

LINDA: All I am asking for is a date. He doesn't have to marry her. Just show enough interest to make her believe there is hope. Just *one* date.

SARAH: What am I supposed to do?

LINDA: Talk to him.

Scene 4

STANLEY, *still in tweed, sits outside at the table under the "Tobacco-Free Campus" sign. He is smoking a cigar, drinking from a coffee mug, and chuckling as he writes on a notepad.* MILTON *enters, also in tweed.*

MILTON: Stanley!

STANLEY (*tossing his pen onto the notepad*): Milton.

MILTON: What trouble are you about?

STANLEY: I have decided to give up women.

MILTON: Entirely?

STANLEY: It seems best — for everyone involved.

MILTON: Is that what you are writing about?

STANLEY: Oh no.

STANLEY *throws* MILTON *the pad of paper.* MILTON *sits next to him, pulls a flask from his jacket pocket, and offers it to* STANLEY. STANLEY *dumps the contents of his mug into a planter and holds out his cup.* MILTON *pours* STANLEY *a bit from the flask and then drinks from the flask himself.*

MILTON (*reading from the notepad*):

> Coastal College seeks a narrow-minded bean counter to serve as its ninth chief academic administrator in as many years. Experience developing programs and policies that stifle initiative, innovation, and imagination is a must. The ideal candidate will show evidence of a sustained commitment to an inefficient and unresponsive bureaucracy that consistently drains funding from core educational programming for the sake of unnecessary administrative bloat. The college encourages applicants whose gender and ethnicity defy modern science.

It is a job description for the new vice president of academic affairs?

STANLEY: Precisely.

MILTON: And how long have you been working on this?

STANLEY: The thought struck me during class.

MILTON: Such a wit must be infinitely satisfying.

STANLEY: Only if I can devise some mischief from it.

MILTON: Did you send it to the hiring committee?

STANLEY: We know that this is precisely the sort of person they are looking for, but they would never post it. Instead, their ad will be full of lies about academic achievement and valuing education.

MILTON: I have an idea. Let's go across the street and discuss it over a drink.

STANLEY: I would love to, but I'm meeting a student in a few minutes.

MILTON: Is she a looker?

STANLEY: Aren't they all?

MILTON: Well, good hunting.

STANLEY: As I said, I am out of the hunt.

MILTON: What makes you think that is best?

STANLEY: I've had two failed marriages. Seems like a sign from the universe.

MILTON: You think your failed marriages are a sign?

STANLEY: That or the hives.

MILTON: Hives?

STANLEY: My Viagra reacts with my cholesterol medicine and gives me hives. The only way I can get an erection is to stop taking the medicine that keeps me alive. I've had to choose: sex or life.

MILTON: You can't have sex if you are dead.

STANLEY: And *I* can't have sex if I am alive.

MILTON: That's quite a dilemma.

STANLEY: And I saw something last week that has me, well, rattled.

MILTON: I am all ears.

STANLEY: A young couple in the apartment across the street — they were having sex and left the curtains open.

MILTON: You saw it?

STANLEY: It was terrifying.

MILTON: I would have advised against watching.

STANLEY: They are so much more…imaginative than I ever was.

MILTON: We grew up with an analog sexuality: centerfolds in secondhand magazines. They grew up with the Internet and Russian snuff porn. Kids these days are all experts.

STANLEY: No wonder my wives were unhappy.

MILTON: I am sure that you made them happy.

STANLEY: Do you really think so?

MILTON: No, but I am your friend. What do you want me to say?

STANLEY: You never question your sexual acumen?

MILTON: As you know, I restrict my romantic adventures to servicing our recently divorced colleagues.

STANLEY: You are doing God's work.

MILTON: These women are juggling two or three kids, a clinically treatable self-esteem problem, and a high-pressure, low-paying university job. They are grateful for any attention — even analog attention.

STANLEY: I don't like the idea that I left both of my wives unsatisfied.

MILTON: Were you satisfied?

STANLEY: Yes, I suppose. But that is the problem, isn't it? Maybe I don't know what real sexual satisfaction is.

MILTON: Trust me, your wives didn't either.

STANLEY: Thanks.

MILTON: You pleased yourself. Any more profound standard is perverse. (*Pause.*) Unless there is something else bothering you.

STANLEY: Me?

MILTON: Are you lonely?

STANLEY: Lonely?

MILTON: You said that you are out of the hunt.

STANLEY: On the contrary, I find myself quite content and enjoying far more leisure time than when I was married.

MILTON: Certainly. If I spent less time servicing our colleagues, I would have more time for reading and reflection.

STANLEY: I recently read an article suggesting that the human brain has a limited number of memory cells and that we waste one cell for every face that we see.

MILTON: Faces?

STANLEY: Yes, for some reason, facial recognition requires a lot of memory.

MILTON: So if you see a lot of faces —

STANLEY: You fill up your memory —

MILTON: And waste your brainpower on facial recognition.

STANLEY: We both know that I haven't much brainpower left. So I have decided not to meet anyone new.

MILTON: How will you teach your classes?

STANLEY: I will stare at the students' feet.

MILTON: That will make our dean happy. She thinks you're a rake who only notices the coeds' décolletage.

STANLEY: Some rake I am. A celibate reduced to staring at women's feet to protect his remaining brain cells.

MILTON: A poor figure we cut.

STANLEY: It is a scurvy world and scurvily we live in it.

MILTON: Where are the days that have been and the seasons that we have seen, when we might sing, swear, drink, think, fornicate, and pontificate as freely as lords?

STANLEY: When the campus was our land, and each year brought a fresh crop for us to harvest.

MILTON: The once proud profession has been reduced to a trade.

STANLEY: I entered academia to pursue a life of the mind.

MILTON: Now we are but cobblers, who cobble together meaningless prattle to convince students to give up their dreams and enter the workforce.

STANLEY: Four years calculated to steal their vitality.

MILTON: There was a time when being a professor meant something. A professor had standing in the community, a sense of decency and dignity. Now, instead of inspiring students to greatness, we are expected to train them to conformity and despair.

STANLEY: And they call it "progress."

MILTON: Imagine how meaningless life must seem when at the age of eighteen your greatest ambition is to get a job.

STANLEY: What happened to a sense of higher purpose?

MILTON: I thought Sarah's new theory was intended to give you a sense of purpose.

STANLEY: Who said that?

MILTON: She did.

STANLEY: Oh God.

MILTON: She's worried about you.

STANLEY: I like purpose perfectly well when giving it to other people, but it has never suited me.

MILTON: I told Sarah that you had been managing your entire life without purpose.

STANLEY: And?

MILTON: She ignored me and pressed upon me the significance of her new discovery.

STANLEY: It is groundbreaking stuff.

MILTON: Long-lost manuscripts from Ivetta of Huy and Saint Catherine of Siena—all suppressed by the church, of course.

STANLEY: She is calling it…"neo-medieval-postmodern-feminism."

MILTON: Catchy.

STANLEY: Apparently, Ivetta proposed that culture programs humans in the same way that biology programs plants and animals. We are all culturally programmed.

MILTON: The medievalists were already postmodernists, eh?

STANLEY: More radical still. These codes show that the patriarchy and the feminist resistance to it are indistinguishable.

MILTON: So these women had already traversed the intellectual corridors that we call postmodern feminism and abandoned it.

STANLEY: By the thousands. They recognized the trap of identity politics and the impossibility of liberation movements. They walked away from their lives and chose devout seclusion.

MILTON: The Beguines?

STANLEY: It means "heretic." They realized that the cultural coding had been perverted and could not be redeemed. They took vows of chastity and silence, and some of them stopped eating. Eventually, Saint Francis of Assisi copied them, and the movement spread to men.

MILTON: Women began the mendicant movement?

STANLEY: Exactly. The mendicant movement was not an escape from sin but an escape from cultural coding — coding that defined everything, including sin. It is quite radical.

MILTON: And recoding —

STANLEY: Is impossible. Once you are in it, you are stuck. You cannot manipulate the social code. Rather, the code manipulates you.

MILTON: So progressive liberalism is…?

STANLEY: Identical to the radical Right.

MILTON: And Christian conservativism?

STANLEY: Indistinguishable from secular humanism.

MILTON: Being a woke vegan is…?

STANLEY: A bourgeois indulgence.

MILTON: Feminism?

STANLEY: An impotent reimagination of a Barbie doll.

MILTON: And the argument is sound?

STANLEY: From what I can tell. Sarah's discovery will change our understanding of culture in the same way Darwin's discovery changed our understanding of biology.

MILTON: Sarah is very bright. The question is…why does she want your help?

STANLEY: She needs a man.

MILTON: Neo-medieval-postmodern-feminism needs a man?

STANLEY: The irony is not lost on her, but some of the Latin manuscripts made their way to the monastery on Mount Athos in Greece.

MILTON: And you read Latin.

STANLEY: Of course. And the Greek priests don't allow women into the monastery, on the mountain, or even onto the peninsula.

MILTON: And there are no copies?

STANLEY: None.

MILTON: So you shall be her proxy?

STANLEY: That is her proposal.

MILTON: Clever.

STANLEY: If she can get the funding.

MILTON: Isn't the dean in charge of those grants?

STANLEY: She is.

MILTON: Linda and Sarah are pals. So long as she leaves your name out of it, Sarah will be fine.

STANLEY: Maybe...but Linda is protective of her brand of feminism, and Sarah's discovery puts it to the sword.

MILTON: No wonder you like it.

STANLEY: I would like to see the dean's face when her life's work is shown to be pointless drivel.

MILTON: Do you think Sarah will put it that way?

STANLEY: When I fantasize about it, she does. Linda is insufferable, and I'd like to see her brought down a peg.

MILTON: I don't care for the way that she finishes other people's sentences—

STANLEY: Incorrectly.

MILTON: For the sake of neo-medieval-postmodern-feminism, let's hope Sarah leaves your name out of it.

STANLEY: I have heard Linda describe me as "everything that is wrong with the university."

MILTON: When she is being charitable. (*He stands and picks up* STANLEY's *notepad.*) May I take this with me?

STANLEY: Of course.

MILTON: I'll be at the bar if you need me.

Act II

Scene 1

> STANLEY *and* TRACY *are seated in* STANLEY's *office.* STANLEY *is smoking a cigar and drinking from a rocks glass.* TRACY *leans forward, gazing at him seductively and twirling her hair.*

TRACY: So, Dr. Stevenson, how long were you and Dr. Sawyer lost in the jungle?

STANLEY: Long enough to explore the variations of destiny.

TRACY: Oh…I, well, I am not sure what that means.

STANLEY: Would you like to discuss it over cocktails?

TRACY: Yes.

STANLEY: Let's walk across the street. Dr. Sawyer is already there. Let me get my coat.

> SARAH *enters, appearing at the door.*

SARAH: Sorry, Stanley hasn't time for drinks this afternoon. He has a prior engagement.

STANLEY (*staring at* SARAH's *feet*): Sarah. Happy to see you. This is, uh —

SARAH: Tracy. Yes, we are acquainted.

TRACY (*sheepishly*): Hi, Professor Morgan.

STANLEY (*to* TRACY): Another time then?

TRACY: OK, Professor.

> TRACY *exits.*

STANLEY: Thank God you arrived. I was on the verge of embarrassing myself.

SARAH: I am not convinced that I arrived soon enough. I overheard your conversation.

STANLEY: Was it bad?

SARAH: Nothing to be proud of.

STANLEY: I am not proud.

SARAH: Then, no harm done — at least not to you.

STANLEY: Is this why you interrupted me? To insult me?

SARAH: I came because…why are you staring at my feet?

STANLEY: Milton and I were discussing —

SARAH: Never mind. I don't want to know. Linda has a proposition for you.

STANLEY: Oh God.

> STANLEY *offers* SARAH *a cigar.*

SARAH: You know this is a tobacco-free campus.

STANLEY *shrugs and puts the cigar back into his shirt pocket.*

SARAH: She would like to see you now.

STANLEY: Now?

SARAH: Now.

STANLEY: Tell her that you found me drunk and incapacitated in my office. I am willing to get drunk quickly if it will help with the deception.

SARAH: The dean is not the harpy you make her out to be.

STANLEY: That is because you don't work for her.

SARAH: Yes, I do.

STANLEY: OK, but it is different. You're a woman.

SARAH: What?

STANLEY: Well, kind of a woman.

SARAH: I beg your pardon.

STANLEY: Well, I mean, you like women.

SARAH: Are you trying to say that I am a lesbian?

STANLEY: I don't like the L-word.

SARAH: I am a lesbian.

STANLEY: I am still not comfortable with that word.

SARAH: Why not?

STANLEY: It is like the M-word.

SARAH: Man?

STANLEY: Marriage. University policy says I can't ask a woman if she is married.

SARAH: But you can say the word.

STANLEY: I can't ask if she is married, is engaged, is pregnant, or has children, presumably because asking if she has children is like asking if she has ever had sex.

SARAH: I don't think that is the reason.

STANLEY: You mean, I can ask a woman if she has had sex?

SARAH: No, you can't ask that either.

STANLEY: How am I intended to speak with women at all?

SARAH: You simply can't talk to women about anything personal.

STANLEY: Milton does.

SARAH: That is because he is *shtuping* them.

STANLEY: So I must *shtup* them before I can ask if they are married?

SARAH: That seems to be Milton's approach.

STANLEY: Now you see why I don't use the L-word.

SARAH: I don't see why you haven't been fired.

STANLEY: It is because I am a philosopher. I am integral to the institution.

SARAH (*shaking her head in disgust*): You are something, all right. But your skills with Latin and Greek make you integral to my research, which is why we need to see Linda.

STANLEY: To secure the grant?

SARAH: Exactly.

STANLEY: I think your chances are better if I am left out of it.

SARAH: You might think, but suddenly, the dean finds that she needs you.

STANLEY: I cannot imagine a world in which her needs align with my own.

SARAH: Be nice. Our grant depends upon it. I texted her and told her to meet us here.

STANLEY: "It" is coming here?

SARAH: It?

STANLEY (*shrugging*): That HR reeducation video recommended we use neutered pronouns.

SARAH (*staring at* STANLEY *and shaking her head*): Neutered?

STANLEY: I think that is what it said. I was drunk when I watched it.

SARAH: That video was my idea.

STANLEY: So why are you asking me to explain it?

SARAH: I was asking you to explain yourself.

STANLEY: What about you? You say you're a les-...les-...that you like women, but I have never seen you with one.

SARAH: I had a girlfriend.

STANLEY: When?

SARAH: In college.

STANLEY: That was twenty years ago!

SARAH: So you had a girlfriend in college and that was thirty years ago. You are still straight.

STANLEY: But I've enjoyed a steady stream of unsuccessful marriages since then.

SARAH: So your unsuccessful heterosexual relationships demonstrate you are heterosexual, but my successful lesbian relationship proves I am not a lesbian?

STANLEY: Yours was successful?

SARAH: Perfectly. We parted ways to pursue our careers.

STANLEY: How do you do it?

SARAH: What?

STANLEY: A successful relationship.

SARAH: It is hard. I don't know that you could manage it.

STANLEY: What is the trick?

SARAH: Care about the other person more than yourself.

STANLEY (*pondering for a bit*): Sarah, why haven't we ever given it a go?

SARAH: A "go"?

STANLEY: Sure.

SARAH (*incredulously*): Because I am a lesbian.

STANLEY: No, really, I am serious.

SARAH: I can't believe you haven't been fired.

STANLEY (*ignoring* SARAH): You are attractive, and you like me more than any other woman I know.

SARAH: Most women over twenty don't like you at all.

STANLEY: Speaking of women who don't like me, what would you like me to say to Linda?

SARAH: Nothing. Please allow me to handle her. This must be done with finesse.

STANLEY: I don't like that you are better with women than I am.

SARAH: I think this is what Linda hopes to cure.

LINDA *enters*.

SARAH: Linda.

LINDA: Sarah. Stanley, how are you?

STANLEY (*looking at* LINDA's *feet*): Still —

LINDA: Chasing coeds?

STANLEY: I was going to say "drunk."

SARAH: Please join us. Stanley was just asking me —

LINDA (*sitting down*): About Helen?

STANLEY: Who?

LINDA: Sarah did not mention Helen?

STANLEY: We were talking about feminism.

LINDA: What do *you* know about feminism?

STANLEY: That I am not allowed to talk about it.

LINDA (*angry*): What?

SARAH (*interrupting*): Linda wants you to meet Helen Mirandari.

LINDA (*composing herself*): Oh yes. Yes.

STANLEY: Who?

LINDA: I know you will like her.

> STANLEY *looks confused. He starts to look up but then looks back down at* LINDA's *feet*.

SARAH (*looking at* STANLEY): He is confused.

LINDA: She is a gender theorist with a joint appointment in the College of Liberal Arts and the Business School.

SARAH (*looking at* LINDA, *then back at* STANLEY): She is trying to set you up on a date.

STANLEY (*continuing to stare at the* LINDA's *feet*): Why me?

LINDA: You will like her.

STANLEY (*finally looking up*): What makes you say that?

> STANLEY *catches himself and looks back down.*

LINDA: Because she is smart.

STANLEY: Smart? You mean "ugly."

SARAH: No. "Nice" means ugly. "Smart" means —

STANLEY: Annoying.

> SARAH *shrugs her shoulders.*

LINDA: She is wonderful, independent, liberated.

STANLEY: Liberated from what?

SARAH: It means she's "easy."

STANLEY: She's easy?

LINDA: She is not "easy."

SARAH: She's kind of cute.

LINDA: Cute?

SARAH: Well, she isn't Ingrid Bergman, but she is what counts for "cute" among university faculty.

LINDA: I can't believe you are calling her "cute." She is a full professor of Gender and —

STANLEY: You had me at "easy."

LINDA: I said "liberated."

STANLEY: Tomato, tomahto. I don't care what sort of professor she is. If she is — how did you say? — "liberated," we will get along great.

LINDA: She's not "easy."

SARAH: She's a feminist.

STANLEY: A feminist?

LINDA: Of course she's a feminist. She is one of the nation's leading scholars in gender and economic theory.

STANLEY: I don't date feminists.

LINDA: Why not?

SARAH: Oh no.

STANLEY: I need a woman who adores men and forgives their faults, not a woman who makes a living critiquing them. Look at me. I can't stand up to that kind of scrutiny.

LINDA: Feminists don't hate men.

STANLEY: They just hate men like me.

LINDA: Well —

STANLEY: I understand first wave feminism and the fight for voting rights, and I appreciate second wave feminism for encouraging women to be more — what did you call it? — "liberated," but modern feminists always dislike me. They use words I don't understand and then look at me with disapproval.

LINDA (*looking at* STANLEY *with disapproval*): Men enjoy a unique set of privileges that allow them to perpetrate violence and economic injustice against women without suffering any repercussions for their actions. How can you hold it against women for pointing this out?

STANLEY: Because they are pointing at me.

SARAH: Can you imagine what Stanley would be without privilege?

LINDA: Homeless?

STANLEY: Exactly. I don't have much to offer a woman. Any woman bent on finding fault with men will find it quickly in me.

LINDA: Maybe this was a bad idea.

SARAH: It was a terrible idea.

STANLEY: I prefer —

LINDA: Younger women?

SARAH: I'll say.

STANLEY: I was going to say —

LINDA: How do you know how old she is?

STANLEY: What?

LINDA: How do you know how old Helen is?

STANLEY: She is a full professor.

LINDA: Yes.

STANLEY: I can only imagine the bloom is off her.

LINDA (*incredulously*): The bloom?

SARAH: He doesn't trust women his own age.

STANLEY: What is wrong with preferring younger women?

LINDA: It is disgusting and immature.

STANLEY: I thought you were a feminist.

LINDA: I am.

STANLEY: Then why do you find young women disgusting?

LINDA: It isn't the women. It is the old men. Why do all middle-aged men like twenty-year-old women?

STANLEY: Perhaps you should ask why twenty-year-old women like middle-aged men?

SARAH: I told you this was a bad idea.

LINDA: An adult man should want a sophisticated woman who enjoys the confidence that comes with maturity.

STANLEY: What is she likely to learn in twenty years?

SARAH: Self-worth?

STANLEY: Cynicism and bitterness.

LINDA: Oh please. You hate intelligent, assertive women.

STANLEY: You mean "cynical" and "bitter" women.

SARAH: Don't engage him.

LINDA: He prefers young women because he can take advantage of them.

SARAH: Wait a minute, Linda. Are you suggesting that young women are unintelligent?

LINDA: No, I am suggesting that they are immature.

SARAH: But you said yourself that Stanley is immature.

LINDA: Shut up.

SARAH: I worry that you dismiss the acuity of young women.

LINDA: Why?

SARAH: You think twenty-year old women should be allowed to have abortions?

LINDA: Of course. I have always been pro-choice.

SARAH: A twenty-year-old woman is mature enough to choose to have an abortion but not mature enough to date Stanley?

LINDA: This was a terrible idea.

SARAH: It was your idea.

LINDA: I promised Helen I would introduce her to someone suitable, someone intelligent.

SARAH: You thought Stanley was "suitable"?

LINDA: I was desperate.

STANLEY: I am fine dating below my station.

LINDA: It is hard to imagine that there is a station below yours.

STANLEY (*standing up and moving toward the door*): On that note, perhaps I should retreat.

LINDA: No, wait!

STANLEY *exits*.

LINDA: What am I going to do? Helen will leave. She is a hot commodity in—

SARAH and LINDA: Gender and economic studies.

SARAH *and* LINDA *both laugh.* STANLEY *returns, lifts his drink, finishes it, and then walks off again without saying anything.* STANLEY *exits*.

LINDA: What was he drinking?

SARAH: A gin and tonic, I think.

LINDA: It isn't even lunchtime yet.

SARAH: That is why he wasn't drinking a martini.

LINDA: But he teaches this afternoon.

SARAH: Don't worry, he will have a martini before class.

LINDA (*thinking for a moment*): Why does he dislike me so much?

SARAH: Because you represent the end of everything he holds dear.

LINDA: You mean "chauvinism," "misogyny," and "white male privilege"?

SARAH: Well...yes. But you must remember that it was Stanley's generation that encouraged diversifying the curriculum, the faculty, and the students. They believed broad participation in higher education would bring with it bold new ideas. What they didn't anticipate is that the new ideas would demonize them and strip the university of its "charm."

LINDA: "Charm"? The universities were havens for social stagnation that indoctrinated the youth to white, male supremacy.

SARAH: If they were so bad, then why were we so desperate to attend them and find employment in them? They were flawed, for sure, but there was some magic in those tweed suits and elbow pads.

LINDA: Misogyny isn't "magic."

SARAH: They knew it, which is why they let us in. But as Stanley sees it, we came and sterilized it.

LINDA: We didn't "sterilize" the university.

SARAH: Didn't we? When I was an undergraduate student, I stayed up until the wee hours with my professors, drinking, smoking, and discussing metaphysics. Now those professors would be pilloried for drinking and fraternizing with students. Under our new, postmodern norms, you utter one thought out of step with the political ideology of the day, and you face a firing squad.

LINDA: Postmodernism simply reveals that Enlightenment values were a ruse for sustaining the patriarchy.

SARAH: Those values justified diversifying the campus in the first place. And though you may not like it, it was men like Stanley who championed diversity.

LINDA: Or was it women like me who demanded inclusion?

They hear voices shouting from offstage.

LINDA: What's that?

SCENE 2

Outside, TRACY stands at a table, megaphone in hand. Behind her, banners read "Conservative Christian Voices for Change," "Abortion Is Murder," and "Christ Was Not a Feminist."

TRACY (*through the megaphone*): Christian women have a right to be heard! Conservative students unite!

SARAH *and* LINDA *enter.*

SARAH: What the hell is this?

LINDA: I have no idea. I didn't authorize a counterprotest.

SARAH: What group is this?

LINDA: I don't know, but they cannot hold a rally without university permission.

SARAH: I suppose not, but I think you would be better off leaving them alone.

LINDA: Why? They have no right to do this.

SARAH: No, Linda, really. (LINDA *approaches* TRACY.) Wait.

LINDA (*to* TRACY): What are you doing here?

TRACY (*still speaking through the megaphone*): We represent the Conservative Christian Campus Crusade!

LINDA: I am right here.

TRACY (*sheepishly*): Sorry.

LINDA: Do you have a rally permit?

TRACY: No. Do we need one?

LINDA: Yes. I am going to have to ask you and your little friend to collect your stuff and leave. Otherwise, I will call security.

MARGOT *enters.*

MARGOT: What is going on?

TRACY: She says we cannot hold a rally without a permit.

MARGOT *whispers into* TRACY's *ear.*

TRACY (*to* LINDA): Who are you?

LINDA: I am the —

SARAH (*grabbing* LINDA *and pulling her away*): This is a bad idea.

LINDA: I am fine. (*She walks back to the table, leaving* SARAH *to watch from a short distance.*) I am the dean of Liberal Arts. You cannot hold a rally without a permit.

MARGOT *whispers in* TRACY's *ear again.*

TRACY: According to the student handbook, a rally is defined as an event that involves more than two people. It is just the two of us, so we don't need a permit.

LINDA: You two don't know what you are talking about.

TRACY: Excuse me?

MARGOT *starts filming with her phone.*

LINDA: This conservative crap crusade is a farce. All your conservative causes are absurd. You think you speak for women, but you don't. You are speaking for the men who have corrupted you: brothers, fathers, boyfriends, and husbands. You enjoy male privilege by association with men, without acknowledging the work feminists did to make your pleasant little lives possible. You wouldn't be allowed at this university if it weren't for generations of women who fought for you, for your rights, and now you betray those women by using the rights they gave you to discredit their efforts.

TRACY: Our fathers corrupted us?

LINDA: That is right. To protect their quaint bourgeois lives built on misogyny and privilege.

MARGOT: It is women like *you* who ruined men. All your "equality" and "marketplace values" have turned romance into a business transaction. If everyone is equal, then love is just a matter of getting the best bang for your buck. You trained men to treat us like commodities — commodities that are too toxic for relationships. Instead of courtship and marriage, we have dating contracts and hookups. We must advertise ourselves on the Internet, on websites where we get swiped right or left, and you call it "liberation."

LINDA: Feminism did not do that to you. It was men — fathers, brothers, husbands — who turned you into a sex object.

TRACY *starts crying.*

LINDA: You think you are fighting for your rights, but you are idiots whose actions threaten to reverse one hundred years of progress.

TRACY *continues to cry, while* MARGOT *keeps filming.*

LINDA: I will not allow this sort of ignorance to go unchallenged.

SARAH (*finally intervening*): Tracy, are you OK?

LINDA (*to* SARAH): You know her?

TRACY (*still crying*): I'm sorry. (*She tries to compose herself.*) Professor Morgen?

SARAH: Yes?

TRACY: You're Professor Stevenson's friend.

LINDA: She knows Stanley?

SARAH: Yes.

LINDA: Oh my God, I should have known. This whole thing was Stanley's idea.

SARAH: This was not Stanley's doing.

LINDA (*furious*): He is trying to ruin my rally.

SARAH: Stanley doesn't care about your rally.

LINDA (*to* TRACY): You and your Conservative Christian Campus Crusade are not welcome here.

TRACY *starts crying again.*

LINDA: I am calling security.

MARGOT: And that's a wrap.

Scene 3

STANLEY *sits at the desk in his office, reading Nietzsche's* Beyond Good and Evil. TRACY *enters.*

TRACY: Professor Stevenson, can I speak with you for a minute?

STANLEY: I have class soon, so just a moment.

TRACY: Did you hear about yesterday's rally?

STANLEY: That god-awful "safe-space" thing? Yes, I heard about it.

TRACY: No, the Conservative Christian Campus Coalition rally.

STANLEY: Oh Jesus, no. Thankfully, I was unaware of it, but it sounds god-awful.

TRACY: It was our rally.

STANLEY: Not mine, I assure you.

TRACY: No, I mean mine, my organization.

STANLEY: You are a member of the Conservative Cramp-ass, uh —

TRACY: Conservative Christian Campus Coalition, yes.

STANLEY: Quite a name.

TRACY: I got in a fight at the rally with one of the professors.

STANLEY: With whom?

TRACY: I am not sure. One of the feminist professors.

STANLEY: I don't suppose your organization can be all bad then.

TRACY: Your friend Dr. Morgan broke it up.

STANLEY: The fight?

TRACY: Yes.

STANLEY: Quite a rally.

TRACY: My friend Margot recorded the whole thing.

STANLEY: Oh. (*He thinks for a moment.*) Oh. (*He thinks a bit more.*) Oh, that could be —

The office phone rings. STANLEY *answers it.*

STANLEY (*into the phone*): Yes. (*Pause.*) Hi, Sarah. (*Pause.*) Yes, I am here. (*Pause.*) Jesus, OK. (*He hangs up.*) Tracy, I must meet Dr. Morgan.

TRACY: But Professor —

STANLEY: Yes?

> TRACY *pauses a moment and fidgets.* SARAH *enters.*

SARAH: Tracy?

TRACY: Professor Morgan.

SARAH: What are you doing here?

TRACY: I was —

SARAH: Just leaving?

TRACY: Yes.

> TRACY *exits.*

STANLEY: That wasn't polite.

SARAH: She hangs around here too much, Stanley.

STANLEY: She is my student.

SARAH: Uh-huh. Anyway, we have a problem.

STANLEY: I am all ears.

SARAH: Linda isn't going to give us the grant unless you ask Helen out on a date.

STANLEY: She said that?

SARAH: No, of course not. But she won't talk about anything else until this Helen thing is settled.

STANLEY: So I need to sleep with Helen to get the grant?

SARAH (*upset*): Stanley.

STANLEY: So this is what it has come to. Used to be it was the women who had to sleep their way to a promotion. I suppose turnabout is fair play.

SARAH (*still upset*): Would you stop, please?

STANLEY: But I must warn you, I haven't had sex in a long time, and from what I can tell, I possess no talent for it. I fear that I may do more harm than good.

SARAH: I never said you had to sleep with her, just ask her out on a date. That is all.

STANLEY: When was the last time you dated, Sarah?

SARAH: Uh, I don't know.

STANLEY: Really?

SARAH: College.

STANLEY: Let me tell you, the dating world has changed since you and I were participants in it. Courtship is dead. It is straight to the bedroom now, and you better bring your A game.

SARAH: *You* have an A game?

STANLEY: No, which is why we are unlikely to get the grant.

SARAH: What are you really worried about, Stanley?

STANLEY: That I will humiliate myself, of course. (*Nervously.*) I don't know anything about modern dating. How do you make a move?

SARAH: A "move"?

STANLEY: Look, it isn't a date unless there is at least a minimal amount of romance, and I was never particularly good at romance. And now, there are so many rules to dating.

SARAH: Good God man, sometimes you just grab the girl and kiss her.

STANLEY: That is not what I have read.

SARAH: You need to read less.

SARAH grabs STANLEY and kisses him hard.

SARAH: Try that!

STANLEY stares at SARAH for a moment, shocked.

SARAH: What? You can manage that, can't you?

STANLEY: I…I…uh…but—

SARAH: What?

STANLEY: I don't have her number.

SARAH (*tossing STANLEY a business card*): Here, call her on her office phone. You can be charming enough when you must. Well, I am telling you — you must.

SARAH turns and walks out of STANLEY's office but then sticks her head back in.

SARAH (*sweetly and blowing him a kiss*): Please.

STANLEY (*blushing*): Get out of here. I need to prepare for class.

SARAH exits. STANLEY removes a small wooden box from a drawer and places it on his desk. He opens the box and retrieves a cigar. He lights the cigar and smokes for a moment, then takes a small cocktail case from the drawer and slowly and carefully makes himself a martini. When he is done, he closes the case ritualistically and leans back, kicking his feet onto the desk. He alternates between puffs of the cigar and sips of the martini.

Scene 4

MILTON *enters* STANLEY's *office, knocking as he walks in.*

MILTON: Stanley.

STANLEY: Milton. Care for a cigar?

MILTON: If you will make me a martini.

STANLEY *opens the cocktail case from the previous scene and repeats his bartending ritual.* MILTON *sees the business card on the desk and picks it up.*

MILTON: Professor Helen Mirandari? Over in Business?

STANLEY: Yeah. You know her?

MILTON: We have never officially met.

STANLEY: Have you seen her?

MILTON: Once, from afar. She's kind of cute. I considered asking her out but —

STANLEY: She has never been married.

MILTON: Precisely. Divorcées are like pre-owned cars. They have plenty of miles left on them, and you pay a fraction of the cost for a new model. I can't afford Helen Mirandari.

STANLEY: You are the last of the romantics.

MILTON: Why her card?

STANLEY: Sarah wants me to ask her out.

MILTON (*laughing*): No, really. Why?

STANLEY: That's it.

MILTON: Sarah wants *you* to date Helen?

STANLEY: To get the grant for Greece, I must navigate a tangled web of academic ambition, feminism, and old-fashioned family values.

MILTON: Stiff price for an academic grant. Why Helen?

STANLEY: Something to do with Helen needing a man to make her happy and Linda needing Helen to be happy in order to secure a promotion.

MILTON: I don't like your chances.

STANLEY: Why?

MILTON: Helen is not your type.

STANLEY: You're telling me.

MILTON: She is a real scholar with a national reputation. What's she likely to see in you?

STANLEY: An object of ridicule.

MILTON: Does Sarah expect you to sleep with her?

STANLEY: I don't know that I'm up to it.

MILTON: Helen Mirandari specializes in the deconstruction of male privilege in the marketplace. Be prepared for some critical analysis afterward.

STANLEY: I don't even know how to ask a woman out. I was never good at it, and now the grant depends on my charisma. This is not likely to succeed.

MILTON (*handing* STANLEY *the business card*): Just dial the number.

STANLEY: What?

MILTON: Dial the number, and put it on speaker.

> STANLEY *presses a button on his office phone, and a dial tone can be heard. He squints at the card as he punches in the number.*

MILTON: Hand me my drink.

> STANLEY *hands* MILTON *his martini as the phone starts to ring. The two wait silently — with* STANLEY's *apprehension a clear contrast to* MILTON's *suave demeanor — until a voice answers.*

HELEN (*via speaker*): Hello.

> MILTON *motions to* STANLEY *to pass him the receiver.* STANLEY *lifts the handset and holds it out to* MILTON.

MILTON: Helen, Stanley Stevenson here, over in Philosophy. We met at the convocation. You were wearing that fabulous gray dress.

STANLEY (*incredulous*): What? I've never —

MILTON (*to* STANLEY, *covering the receiver*): Flattery always works.

STANLEY: But how do you remember what she was wearing?

MILTON: I always make a point of remembering what women are wearing. (*He uncovers the receiver.*) No, no, you won't remember me. You were surrounded by admirers, and the dean wouldn't let you out of her sight.

STANLEY: You are a genius!

MILTON (*ignoring* STANLEY): Helen, as you may know, Dr. Morgan and I are working on a new thesis regarding feminism and cultural coding. I was hoping to get your feedback on some of these ideas.

STANLEY: An evil genius.

MILTON: I hate meeting in the office to discuss business. Would you be willing to meet me for drinks this afternoon?

STANLEY: Do you practice?

MILTON *gestures to* STANLEY *to pass him a cigar.* STANLEY *quickly lights one and hands it to* MILTON. *He savors the draw and then blows the smoke slowly across the room.*

MILTON: OK. (*Pause.*) OK. (*Pause.*) That sounds even better. I am looking forward to it.

MILTON *passes the receiver to* STANLEY, *who hangs it up.*

MILTON: You are meeting her at her place for dinner tonight.

STANLEY: Dinner? At her place? I thought you said "drinks."

MILTON: She said that such a discussion was likely to last longer than a drink and suggested that I — I mean "you" — come over for dinner instead.

STANLEY: Jesus Christ.

MILTON: I have complete confidence in you.

STANLEY: I am going to have to sleep with her.

MILTON *finishes his drink, sets the cigar in an ashtray on* STANLEY'*s desk, and walks to the door.*

MILTON: You might want to bring the appropriate accoutrements.

STANLEY: Accoutrements?

MILTON: A toothbrush.

STANLEY: Jesus Christ.

MILTON: And your A game.

MILTON *exits.*

STANLEY (*yelling across his empty office*): I don't have an A game!

STANLEY *sits, smokes his cigar for a moment, and then finishes his martini. He immediately begins making another.*

SCENE 5

SARAH enters STANLEY's office and finds him — cigar and drink in hand — lost in thought. She sets the small bag that she is carrying in an empty chair.

SARAH (*slyly*): I thought you had class.

STANLEY (*earnestly looking at his watch and placing his drink on the desk*): I do. So make it quick.

SARAH (*holding back her excitement*): You did it!

STANLEY: What?

SARAH (*doing a little dance*): You got us the grant. You are my hero. I could kiss you!

SARAH leans on STANLEY's desk, dangerously close to the rocks glass and his cocktail case.

STANLEY (*shielding his cocktail setup with his arms*): Don't! You might overturn my drink.

SARAH (*reaching across the desk and kissing STANLEY squarely on the lips*): I didn't think you were going to do it, and then you go and surprise everyone.

STANLEY (*clearly unsettled*): What the hell?

SARAH: You asked Helen out on a date.

STANLEY: What? How could you possibly know? Is my office bugged?

SARAH: Small campus. News travels fast.

STANLEY: I'll say.

SARAH: Linda was in Helen's office when you called. Apparently, she told Linda the whole thing.

STANLEY: Jesus Christ.

SARAH: Are you kidding? This is the best thing that could happen to us. Apparently, you were incredibly charming. Linda couldn't believe it. No one thought you had it in you.

STANLEY: Thanks.

SARAH: She came straight to my office, told me about your date, and then explained that she is a shoo-in to be the next vice president.

STANLEY: This won't work.

SARAH: Are you kidding? It has already worked! HR called Linda and told her that the ad for the new VP has been posted and that she is their number one candidate.

STANLEY: The ad wasn't supposed to come out for days.

SARAH: Who cares? It's out, and Linda's in. I mentioned the grant, and she said that she would expedite it. We are going to Greece!

SARAH resumes her dance and then kisses STANLEY again, despite his protests.

STANLEY (*flustered by SARAH's advances and his realization*): Yeah, and I am going to have to sleep with Helen.

SARAH: Sleep with her?

STANLEY: That is what Milton said.

SARAH: Just be a gentleman, please! I know you have it in you. One simple date. That is all I ask. Just think of Greece and how famous we will be.

STANLEY: For God and Greece!

SARAH: Something like that.

STANLEY: It's a good thing for you that I have no scruples. Imagine if the dean had asked one of the women on the faculty to go on a date with a man to benefit her career.

SARAH: You know perfectly well that you cannot apply a moral principle to someone else if you don't believe in it yourself. Have you become a prude, Professor Stevenson?

STANLEY: Fine, I will do it, but it is time for my class.

SARAH: Cancel it. We are going to celebrate. I'm buying.

SARAH pulls a bottle of brown liquor from her bag. STANLEY shrugs, finishes his drink, and sets another rocks glass on his desk.

STANLEY: I suppose I have earned it.

SARAH pours two drinks.

Act III

Scene 1

    STANLEY's *office is dark. A cell phone rings, illuminating the desk and the empty rocks glass in which the phone sits, discarded and forgotten. After a moment, the ringing stops. It starts again and then ceases completely.*

SARAH: What the hell is that?

STANLEY: What?

SARAH: That sound?

STANLEY: I think it's a phone.

SARAH: Where am I?

STANLEY: Please stop yelling.

SARAH: I am not yelling.

STANLEY: My head says otherwise.

Offstage and at a distance, LINDA *can be heard banging on a door and shouting, "Sarah. Sarah?" She pauses and then knocks on another door, slightly closer. Eventually, she enters* STANLEY's *office and turns on the lights.* STANLEY *and* SARAH *are tangled together on the floor, mostly still dressed but disheveled, shoes and accessories strewn about them. Three empty liquor bottles haphazardly lie on the desk, near the rocks glass with the cell phone and second one that is overturned.*

LINDA: What is going on here?

SARAH (*to* STANLEY): Why don't you lock your office door?

STANLEY (*looking at her feet*): Shh. Maybe "it" will go away if we don't answer.

LINDA (*to* SARAH): Why aren't you answering your phone? I have been trying to reach you.

SARAH: Because I am —

LINDA: In trouble?

SARAH: Hungover.

STANLEY: What time is it?

LINDA: It's twelve.

SARAH: Twelve?

LINDA: Sorry, twelve thirty.

SARAH: At night?

LINDA: In the afternoon.

SARAH: What day is it?

STANLEY: I think it's tomorrow.

SARAH: Oh God.

STANLEY: Where are my pants?

LINDA: Did you two sleep together?

STANLEY (*to* SARAH): What is "it" talking about?

SARAH: What do you want, Linda?

LINDA: What do I want? I will tell you what I want. I want — wait — wait a minute. I thought Stanley was supposed to be on a date with Helen last night.

SARAH: He —

STANLEY: Who?

SARAH: You forgot?

LINDA: You forgot?

STANLEY (*motioning to the empty bottles*): I drank all of that. You can't expect me to account for my actions.

LINDA: I don't know what to say. Could this day get any worse?

SARAH: It would get better if you left.

LINDA: That would not solve our problem.

SARAH: Our problem?

LINDA: You obviously don't know, do you?

STANLEY: I am glad that I am not the only one who never knows what women are talking about.

LINDA: Those girls.

SARAH: What girls?

LINDA: Those wretched little girls at the rally. Stanley's friends.

SARAH: Yes?

LINDA: They recorded the whole thing.

SARAH: Our conversation?

STANLEY: What rally?

LINDA: The Conservative Christian Campus crap fest or some such thing.

STANLEY: "Crap fest." That's funny.

SARAH: I think "coalition" is the word you are —

LINDA: Whatever. They posted the video, and it has gone viral. Everyone has seen it. The governor has seen it.

SARAH: The governor?

LINDA: He called the board of regents this morning demanding our resignation.

STANLEY gets up, slowly and painfully, and sits at his desk. He types something on his computer.

SARAH: Our resignation?

LINDA: Immediately.

SARAH: On what grounds?

LINDA: For intimidating students. They don't think that the campus is safe for conservative students, and they see this video as proof of their long-held suspicion.

STANLEY apparently finds what he is searching for, and a recording of LINDA's shouting from the rally can be heard.

STANLEY: This is not good.

SARAH stands up and joins STANLEY. She grimaces at the computer screen.

SARAH: This is horrible.

LINDA: For years, the conservatives have accused us of being radical liberals indoctrinating students to communism and undermining Christian values.

STANLEY (*chuckling, then coughing, and chuckling again*): This may be all the proof they need.

SARAH: What have we done?

STANLEY: Two professors threatening to throw two Christians girls off campus for, well, being Christians.

LINDA: That is not what happened.

STANLEY: That's what it looks like.

SARAH: We are going to face a firing squad.

LINDA: I know.

SARAH: We are about to become the poster children for feminism run amok.

LINDA: And it's Stanley's fault.

STANLEY (*looking up, then quickly back down at* LINDA's *feet*): Excuse me?

LINDA: That girl…you put her up to this, didn't you?

STANLEY: What?

LINDA: You have held a grudge against me for years.

STANLEY: Well, you have been —

LINDA: Trying to protect the coeds from you?

STANLEY: I was going to say "writing me poor performance reviews."

LINDA: Because you don't perform.

STANLEY (*pointing to his computer*): Is this your idea of performance?

SARAH: Linda, surely you can't believe that Stanley encouraged them.

LINDA: Why not? He is part of their, what did you call it, "coalition."

STANLEY: I am not —

LINDA: He is the epitome of misogyny and white male privilege. I am sure he would do anything he could to strike a blow against strong women.

SARAH: Linda, Stanley is an ass, but he isn't that sort of ass.

LINDA: Then whose idea was it?

SARAH: The video was posted by Tracy.

LINDA: His friend.

STANLEY: Student.

LINDA (*to* STANLEY): That you sleep with.

STANLEY: With whom I sleep.

LINDA: What?

STANLEY: You ended the sentence with a preposition.

LINDA: And you are a sexual predator.

STANLEY: It seems the coeds prefer sexual predators to feminists.

LINDA: You are everything that is wrong with this place. You should be fired.

STANLEY: Despite my rakishness, it is you who faces a sacking.

SARAH: Linda, perhaps we should —

LINDA: Resign? No way. I —

SARAH: I was going to say "apologize." We made the girl cry.

LINDA: I am not apologizing to one of Stanley's sluts.

STANLEY: You mean "liberated."

LINDA: We need to come up with a strategy to deal with this straight away. I am going to my office to call my attorney. I suggest you do the same. I intend to have those girls expelled, I intend to be promoted, and I intend to continue to advocate for women's issues on this campus.

LINDA turns and exits. SARAH sits down. There is a moment of silence.

SARAH: What am I going to do?

STANLEY: Don't ask me. I never know the right thing to do.

SARAH: I don't believe you. Can't you…can't you…(*She stands and looks at* STANLEY *for a moment.*) You know her.

STANLEY: Who?

SARAH: Tracy. (*She continues to stare, briefly lost in thought.*) You could—

STANLEY: What?

SARAH: Never mind. It's my problem, not yours.

Before STANLEY *can respond,* SARAH *grabs her shoes and her phone and exits.*

STANLEY: What?

STANLEY buries his face in his hands. MILTON *enters, nattily dressed and a clear contrast to* STANLEY's *unkempt attire.*

MILTON: *Care este problema?*

STANLEY (*not looking up*): Sorry, my Romanian is crap.

MILTON: What is wrong? Why the sad face?

STANLEY: Sarah could be fired.

MILTON (*sitting*): I will need a full explanation. But given the daytime hour and the slight hangover I am carrying from last night's exertions, a cigar and a cup of coffee are in order. Have you any coffee?

STANLEY: No. You know, when I started at this university, the secretary would bring us coffee.

MILTON: Those days are long gone.

STANLEY: Will bourbon and a cigar answer?

MILTON: I suppose it must.

STANLEY hands MILTON a box of cigars and a lighter, then turns the bottles on the desk searching for remnants. He finds one with some liquor left and splits it between two glasses. MILTON takes a moment to light two cigars, passes one to STANLEY, and then accepts a glass of bourbon in exchange.

MILTON: So Sarah is to be sacked. Could the fact that you are wearing the same suit of clothes today have anything to do with her troubles?

STANLEY: No.

MILTON: But you did sleep with her last night, didn't you?

STANLEY: No.

MILTON: Don't be coy with me. I saw her leaving. Like you, she is wearing the same clothes she wore yesterday.

STANLEY: How is it you are so observant of people's clothing?

MILTON: I have taken your advice. I have stopped looking at faces. Despite drinking myself into oblivion last night, I can see everything with perfect clarity.

STANLEY: At least it is working for one of us.

MILTON (*shrugging and puffing on his cigar*): So you and Sarah spent the night together?

STANLEY: It's not what you think.

MILTON: And now she is being fired.

STANLEY: Yes.

MILTON: Seems a stiff penalty for an office shag.

STANLEY: We didn't —

MILTON: Well, this is no good....No good at all....She is the only one in our department who does any meaningful work. You know that our annual budget is based on overall production?

STANLEY: I know.

MILTON: She teaches the big freshman seminars.

STANLEY: Yes.

MILTON: She publishes in the best academic journals.

STANLEY: Yes.

MILTON: She serves on the faculty senate, the curriculum committee, the accreditation committee —

STANLEY: OK, OK, I get it. She does all the work around here.

MILTON: What sort of trouble is she in?

STANLEY shows MILTON the video. MILTON watches it only for an instant before leaning back in his chair and smoking his cigar for a while.

MILTON: This is bad. I imagine our dean is in some hot water as well.

STANLEY: She is. The governor has demanded that they both resign.

MILTON: The dean will wiggle out of it. Deans always do. But Sarah—

STANLEY: Won't be so lucky.

MILTON: But isn't the girl on the video your student?

STANLEY: Yeah.

MILTON: So…

STANLEY (*pausing*): What are you suggesting?

MILTON: Nothing. (*He pauses, continues to smoke, and then provocatively leans forward.*) Unless there is something to suggest.

STANLEY: Out with it.

MILTON: Maybe you could talk to her.

STANLEY: Talk to her?

MILTON: What harm would it do?

STANLEY: Just talk to her?

MILTON: I didn't say that. I recommend you take whatever steps you think necessary to secure Sarah's pardon.

STANLEY: You want me to seduce her?

MILTON: Romance may not be your forte, but it may be all that stands between Sarah and the postmodern chaos.

STANLEY: Who do you think I am?

MILTON: Yesterday you agreed to have sex with a middle-aged economist to secure a travel grant. I think I have the measure of you.

STANLEY: Yeah, but—

MILTON: You will seduce an economist for money, but you won't seduce a coed to save a friend? Is this what you teach in your ethics class?

STANLEY: I can't.

MILTON: You can't teach ethics?

STANLEY: I can't seduce the coed.

MILTON: Why not?

STANLEY: You know I can't....I haven't managed to "rise to the occasion" in years.

MILTON *leans back and smokes.*

STANLEY: My sinister reputation is a ruse.

MILTON: Uh-huh.

STANLEY: I am but a pseudo-libertine, playing the part of the rogue to conceal an impotent existence.

MILTON: Let's hope Sarah has a good attorney. She finds herself between Scylla and Charybdis: between an anti-intellectual conservativism and a pseudo-intellectual progressivism.

MILTON *stands and finishes his drink.*

STANLEY: Do your students understand you when you teach?

The office phone rings, but STANLEY *does not move to answer it. A voice-mail system eventually responds.* STANLEY's *outgoing message can be heard: "'There are no dangerous thoughts; thinking itself is dangerous.' It is likely unwise to leave a message."*

HELEN (*on the phone*): Stanley, I just wanted to thank you for last night. For the great conversation and, well, you know. Thanks. See you soon.

MILTON: And you said you couldn't "rise to the occasion." I am impressed, and apparently, Sarah was, too.

STANLEY (*looking perplexed and glaring at the phone*): That wasn't from Sarah.

MILTON: You dog. Who was it?

STANLEY: I don't know.

MILTON: Could it have been the coed?

STANLEY: Highly unlikely.

MILTON: Pity. Then Sarah's troubles might be over. (*He places his glass on* STANLEY's *desk and walks to the door.*) I suggest you summon whatever magic you used on the girl who left that message to save Sarah's job.

Scene 2

SARAH *is sitting outside at a table, staring at her cell phone.* MILTON *enters, though he does not make eye contact with* SARAH.

MILTON: What are people to think of lesbians if they keep sleeping with the men on this campus?

SARAH: That we are as desperate as the heterosexual women.

MILTON: The pickings are slim.

SARAH: You have no idea.

MILTON: I might know more than you think.

SARAH: What do you mean?

MILTON: The reason Linda is single.

SARAH: Why?

MILTON: Did you ask her.

SARAH: I did. She said she quit trying.

MILTON: She was still trying when I arrived here.

SARAH: Oh….She didn't tell me…but I guessed as much.

MILTON: Only Stanley knows.

SARAH: Which is why she hates both of you.

MILTON: No, I think she hates Stanley because of his politics.

SARAH: You mean, his distaste for pluralism and diversity?

MILTON: Is it really pluralism if she calls the police the moment she encounters an opinion that differs from her own?

SARAH: You saw the video.

MILTON: I don't mind it. This campus needs a bit more of the rough-and-tumble.

SARAH: That doesn't seem to be the opinion of the governor or the board of regents.

MILTON: They are nincompoops.

SARAH: Nincompoops who can fire faculty.

MILTON: Are you to be sacked?

SARAH: Yes.

   SARAH's *phone rings. She answers it.*

SARAH: Hi, Linda. (*There is a long pause.*) Uh-huh. (*Another long pause.*) OK. (*She hangs up.*)

MILTON: Good news?

SARAH: The governor has recommended the closing of the Gender and Women's Studies Program.

MILTON: Why?

SARAH: Someone told him that one of the instigators, me, has a joint appointment in Gender and Women's Studies.

MILTON: That seems drastic.

SARAH: They see that program as a hotbed of anti-Christian, anti-family, anti-conservative values.

MILTON: The universities should be hotbeds — hotbeds for everything! Lively places full of iconoclasm and heresy, not sterile nursing homes for the youth.

SARAH: Shouldn't they be safe spaces for learning?

MILTON: The youth don't need safety. They need adventure. The university experience offers students four years to immerse themselves in the cauldron of culture: intellectually, metaphysically, and corporeally.

SARAH: Corporeally?

MILTON: Sexually.

SARAH: They don't want culture anymore. They want job training.

MILTON: Virtually every meaningful aspect of human life has been forsaken to the gods of standardization, conformity, and efficiency. Must their education be sacrificed as well?

SARAH: Policymakers believe there is a liberal conspiracy on campus committed to spreading communism and atheism.

MILTON: And this video provides them with all the evidence they need, I suppose.

SARAH: To be fair, the girls' video is accurate. We made our own bed.

MILTON: Isn't Stanley chummy with one of these girls?

SARAH: Another reason Linda hates him.

MILTON: Did you tell him how you feel about him?

SARAH: Who?

MILTON: Stanley?

SARAH: I am about to be fired. I am not thinking about Stanley right now.

SARAH's phone rings again.

SARAH: It's Linda. (*She answers it.*) Yes? (*Pause.*) What? (*Pause.*) I am not sure that is a good idea. (*Pause.*) Why don't we just talk to her? (*A long pause.*) I think this is a big mistake. (*Pause.*) All right, fine. (*She hangs up the phone.*)

MILTON: Linda plans to sue the girls?

SARAH: How did you know?

MILTON: I am doing this thing Stanley taught me, where I don't make —

SARAH: Eye contact? Yes, he told me about it. He said it was *your* idea.

MILTON: I can't remember. Great minds —

SARAH: Uh-huh.

MILTON: I understand everything that is going on around me, with perfect clarity and vision.

SARAH: OK, genius, then what am I supposed to do?

MILTON: Tell Stanley how you feel.

SARAH: I am talking about getting fired or, preferably, avoiding it.

MILTON: I think Stanley is more important.

SARAH: What? I don't care about Stanley. I care about my job — the job I may not have by the end of this week if I don't do something.

MILTON: Have you ever tried?

SARAH (*annoyed*): What?

MILTON: Telling him the truth?

SARAH: Why are we talking about Stanley?

MILTON: Humor me.

SARAH (*exasperated*): Yes, fine, OK. I wanted to tell him. Once.

MILTON: When?

SARAH: After his divorce.

MILTON: So why didn't you?

SARAH: I was waiting. Waiting for the right amount of time to pass, waiting until it seemed appropriate.

MILTON: And?

SARAH: By the time I got around to it, he was engaged.

MILTON: So?

SARAH: I generally don't like to seduce a man immediately after meeting his fiancée.

MILTON: He's not engaged now.

SARAH: That is because he is too busy seducing students in his office.

MILTON: And lesbians.

SARAH: Shut up.

MILTON: You should talk to him.

SARAH: Because we spent the night in his office?

MILTON: Because you fancy him. And from what I have heard, he is quite the lover.

SARAH: Stanley?

MILTON: Who would have thunk it? But if you heard the message on his machine today —

SARAH: Message?

MILTON: From a lady friend.

SARAH: Oh God. I don't want to know.

MILTON: I thought you didn't care.

SARAH: I don't.... Who was it?

MILTON: I don't know. You know Stanley as well as I.

SARAH: You two have been friends since college.

MILTON: OK, but he confides in you. I thought you might know the mystery woman.

MILTON takes two cigars from his jacket and offers SARAH one.

SARAH (*declining in a distracted fashion*): I didn't even know he was dating. Unless it is Tracy, the student who hangs around his office —

MILTON: And?

SARAH: Made the video.

MILTON (*lighting a cigar*): That is what I was hoping.

SARAH: Ew. That is gross.

MILTON: It might solve your problem.

SARAH: You are disgusting.

MILTON shrugs.

SARAH: You think Stanley can...*talk* this girl into changing her mind about the incident yesterday?

MILTON: He's a good talker, and if that message on his machine is anything to go by, he has a better chance than the dean's attorney.

SARAH: So it has come to this. My academic career and the fate of the Gender and Women's Studies Program hinging on the charms of a mediocre, middle-aged man.

MILTON: Let's hope he can "rise to the occasion."

Scene 3

TRACY sits outside at a table. She is drinking a soda and watching the video on her phone. MARGOT enters with a backpack and a drink of her own. She sees TRACY and joins her.

MARGOT: Now you know why I record everything.

TRACY: It has been shared thousands of times.

MARGOT: The governor has seen it.

TRACY: I was wearing that flowered dress.

MARGOT: You are famous! A hero to our cause. A martyr like, uh, like Jesus.

TRACY: Never wear patterns on camera. I look like a cow.... What cause?

MARGOT: Overthrowing the liberal propagandists who control universities. Firing that Gender Studies professor is a good first step.

TRACY: Are they planning to fire her?

MARGOT: That's what I hear.

TRACY: But it was the dean who was so horrid.

MARGOT: Yeah, deans don't get fired. They get promoted.

TRACY: Why?

MARGOT: Nobody knows for sure, but from what I have gleaned in my business courses, advancement in administration is inversely proportional to effectiveness.

TRACY: So only Professor Morgan will be fired.

MARGOT: Oh no, we may get the entire Liberal Arts program shut down, and then they will get the dean, too.

TRACY: How?

MARGOT: You know Reverend Peter Toucher?

TRACY: The megachurch guy on TV?

MARGOT: He saw the video. He wants to meet with you.

TRACY: Why me?

MARGOT: He is a personal friend of the governor's. He thinks we can use this incident to eliminate all the humanities departments.

TRACY: Entirely?

MARGOT: He is impressed with you and thinks that you can become the face of the anti-elitist movement. (*She shouts as if at a rally.*) Down with the liberal elite!

TRACY: But I'm a liberal arts major.

MARGOT: But they don't really teach you anything, do they?

TRACY: What do you mean?

MARGOT: It's just anti-Christian, anti-American propaganda taught by communists, atheists, and feminists.

TRACY: Stanley isn't, I mean, Professor Stevenson isn't —

MARGOT: He's a Christian?

TRACY: Well no, I don't think so, but he dislikes feminism and what he calls "nihilistic egalitarianism."

MARGOT: Nihilistic egalitarianism?

TRACY: That in advanced capitalist societies egalitarian movements invariably reduce everyone to objects.

MARGOT: What does that mean?

TRACY: I don't really know....But he said that the university encouraged women to come onto campus and then created rules restricting the interaction between men and women.

MARGOT: You mean, told *him* not to take advantage of them.

TRACY: Professor Stevenson?

MARGOT: He's a predator.

TRACY: If women and men are equal, why do women need protection from men?

MARGOT: Because the patriarchy sustains systemic misogyny and rape culture.

TRACY: I thought you said that Christians support the patriarchy.

MARGOT: No, we support the *Christian* patriarchy. Professor Stevenson is not a Christian.

TRACY: Oh.

MARGOT: We will show them that it isn't safe to be a Christian on this campus, and then we can get rid of the Liberal Arts College and professors like Dr. Stevenson.

TRACY: What did he do?

MARGOT: Reverend Toucher will bring this university to its knees.

TRACY: What about me?

MARGOT: I am arranging another rally today. Can you come?

TRACY: I don't know.

MARGOT: You've got to. Reverend Toucher will be there.

> MARGOT *exits.* TRACY *sits a moment, then takes out her phone, and sends a text. She gets up and exits.*

Scene 4

> LINDA *enters and approaches the table* MARGOT *and* TRACY *just vacated. She is carrying a big cup of coffee. Her phone rings.*

LINDA: Dean Thompson speaking. (*Pause.*) Yes. (*Pause.*) Yes, that is right. That is right. (*Pause.*) Well, that is wonderful news. Thank you.

> LINDA *hangs up the phone and sits down, looking self-satisfied.* MILTON *enters but does not make eye contact with* LINDA.

MILTON: Hello, Linda. You look pleased with yourself this afternoon.

LINDA: I am.

MILTON: Nothing I can fix, I trust?

LINDA: Oh no. My contentment has nothing at all to do with you.

MILTON: I shouldn't imagine. Do you plan to share your —

LINDA: Good news?

MILTON: Table?

LINDA: No.

MILTON *sits anyway.* LINDA *snorts with derision.*

MILTON: I heard you were to be sacked.

LINDA: Oh no. My attorney straightened that out.

MILTON: The new video recording law?

LINDA: You know?

MILTON: It should have occurred to me before, but the law is new.

LINDA: The governor signed it into law last week. There was a big ceremony and everything. Video or audio recording of a state, county, or city employee — without their written permission — is inadmissible as evidence in a court of law or for professional disciplinary decisions.

MILTON: Designed to protect police from videos showing them using excessive force.

LINDA: The governor calls police the "thin blue line" between us and anarchy, crime, and chaos.

MILTON: Thin blue line indeed. Now a thin (MILTON *looks up at* LINDA's *clothing*) black line.

LINDA: Well, he can't force my resignation using a video that breaks a law he signed last week without looking like an idiot.

MILTON: And Gender and Women's Studies?

LINDA: That program is not out of the woods.

MILTON: Because an academic program is not a state employee.

LINDA: Precisely. The board of regents has seen the video, and it has provided them with all the support they need to do what they want.

MILTON: Shutter the Gender and Women's Studies Program?

LINDA: Shutter the entire Liberal Arts College.

MILTON: What?

LINDA: The regents have wanted to eliminate the liberal arts here for years. They prefer job training.

MILTON: And a purging of the campus liberals.

LINDA: It's a win-win for them.

MILTON: But you are the dean of Liberal Arts. The Gender and Women's Studies Program is your baby. Why aren't you upset?

LINDA: Oh, I am upset.

MILTON: I have seen you upset, and this isn't it.

LINDA *scowls at* MILTON.

LINDA (*to herself*): Maybe it was time.

MILTON: To lose the College of Liberal Arts?

LINDA: The university must evolve.

MILTON: I suppose understanding the foundations of civilization has gone out of fashion?

LINDA: The dinosaurs did not evolve, so they went extinct. The liberal arts must evolve.

MILTON: How are they to evolve if they are eliminated?

LINDA: *You* are a dinosaur. It is you who will go extinct.

MILTON: We are constructing an empire of stupidity — devoid of any intellectual virtue and justifying this commitment to ignorance by calling it "progress." If I become extinct for refusing to participate in this vulgarity, then so be it.

LINDA: You will become extinct because you are a drunk and a womanizer. You are a creature of an age long past. The universities are changing, and your type is not part of the plan.

MILTON: Civilization was built by womanizing drunkards. I don't know how you will manage without us.

LINDA: I think history will show that we managed quite nicely.

MILTON: There won't be any History. That department will be eliminated along with Literature, French, German, Economics —

LINDA: Not Economics. Economics will be moved to the Business School.

MILTON: Then I am saved.

LINDA: Oh. (*Disappointed.*) Oh damn.

MILTON: You recall?

LINDA (*still disappointed*): Yes.

MILTON: I hold a joint appointment in Philosophy and Economics —

LINDA: With fake PhDs from that fictional university in…where was it?

MILTON: Transylvania.

LINDA: I thought it was in Romania.

MILTON: It is.

LINDA: I don't believe it's real.

MILTON: I assure you, Romania is real.

LINDA: I meant the university.

MILTON: No, it closed when Romania joined the EU.

LINDA: Yes, I have heard your story. Quite convenient. Now that it is closed, there is no proof you didn't attend.

MILTON: I have a diploma —

LINDA: Which is certainly forged.

   MILTON *shrugs.*

LINDA: And I am supposed to believe you speak Romanian?

MILTON: Romanian is a simple language. If you have Latin and Italian, you have Romanian.

LINDA: And you have Latin and Italian?

MILTON: Don't all educated people?

LINDA: Can you prove it?

MILTON: Ask me any question you like in Romanian.

LINDA: I don't speak Romanian.

MILTON: Latin or Italian?

LINDA: No.

MILTON: Then you must take my word for it.

LINDA: You have nothing to show for your economics education except a piece of paper.

MILTON: My dear, a piece of paper is no evidence of an education. A man demonstrates his education in the way he carries himself, in the manner of his speech, in the interest which others show for what he says and writes.

LINDA: A man?

MILTON (*correcting himself*): I'm sorry, an *educated* man. An educated man is someone whose company is sought by educated men. When I was interviewed for the position in the Economics Department, I —

LINDA: Bullshitted them?

MILTON: Demonstrated my education by the quality of my discourse on the nationalizing of the stock market.

LINDA: That makes no sense.

MILTON: Precisely. Our private markets are now fully financed by the federal government. Anytime there is a danger of a market decline — or significant losses at the banks — the feds pour money into the market, generally through quantitative easing, which is just a fancy term for "printing money." That's a socialized market.

LINDA: So your job is safe.

MILTON: So it seems, but the Philosophy Department is doomed. Sarah, Stanley —

LINDA: I can't say I am sorry to lose Stanley, but he served his purpose.

MILTON: Purpose?

LINDA: Dr. Mirandari called the search committee this morning and recommended me for the provost position.

MILTON: How is that possible?

LINDA: Because she holds me in very high esteem.

MILTON: No, I mean, the ad went out yesterday. The search committee is already making recommendations?

LINDA: I am an outstanding candidate. I was told I am their first choice.

MILTON: All because of Stanley's —

LINDA: Charms? Yes, I admit, he surprised me.

MILTON: I thought to say "his job description."

LINDA: What job description?

MILTON: It is not important. I am sure that Stanley swept Dr. Mirandari off her feet.

LINDA: I don't know that I would go that far.

MILTON: You should give credit where credit is due.

LINDA: He is obviously more of a gentleman than you.

MILTON: I think I am precisely the gentleman he is. I wonder why you did not think to introduce me to Dr. Mirandari.

LINDA: You?

MILTON: Why not? Lots of women like me.

LINDA (*standing*): Ew. Women like Helen dislike men like you, and when I am provost, perhaps I will finally be able to do something about that.

LINDA *exits.*

MILTON (*to himself*): You already have.

MILTON *exits in the opposite direction.*

Scene 5

STANLEY *sits at his desk in his office, making a drink in a cocktail shaker.* MILTON *enters.*

MILTON (*sitting in a swivel chair facing the desk*): You are an evil genius.

STANLEY: How's that?

MILTON: That fake job description you wrote for the provost position.

STANLEY: Yes, my best academic work in years.

MILTON: It worked all right.

STANLEY: What are you talking about?

MILTON: I posted it.

STANLEY: What? How?

MILTON: Oh, it was simple enough. Ever since the university shifted to two-factor authentication for passwords, hacking the system is as simple as "kiss my hand."

STANLEY: Care for a drink?

MILTON: I thought you would never ask.

STANLEY *fetches a second glass, pours two cocktails, and hands one to* MILTON.

STANLEY: So the ad I wrote is posted.

MILTON: Not only is that the ad that is currently running, but apparently HR thought Linda was well suited to it.

STANLEY: Linda got the job.

MILTON: Not yet, but she is now their first choice, all thanks to you.

STANLEY: They really liked the ad?

MILTON: I doubt they bothered to read it. I doubt Linda read it. But it may be that — because of that absurd ad — no one else applied.

STANLEY: So that is how she will get the job?

MILTON: That is my theory, and it is certainly better than Linda's.

STANLEY: Linda has a theory?

MILTON: She believes that it was a phone call to the committee from Helen that earned her the spot.

STANLEY: Oh shit.

MILTON: What?

STANLEY: I was supposed to go out with Helen last night.

MILTON: I anticipated your memory impotence. You've been looking at too many faces.

STANLEY: What did you do?

MILTON: I went to Helen's house for dinner.

STANLEY: But she was expecting me.

MILTON: She hasn't met you.

STANLEY: So?

MILTON: So anyone could have arrived and pretended to be you.

STANLEY: That's why she called…me. She thought—

MILTON: Yes?

STANLEY: She thought I was you.

MILTON: Not exactly.

STANLEY: She thought you were me?

MILTON: Fortunately, most women are not very particular when it comes to men.

STANLEY: And she was happy.

MILTON: I gather—from the message she left on your machine—that she was very happy.

STANLEY: You, you, you slept with her.

MILTON: I was just trying to help.

STANLEY: I am amazed. I've never received such a satisfied response from a lover.

MILTON: Now you have.

STANLEY: Hardly.

MILTON: Well, she still thinks she slept with you. I say that counts.

STANLEY: Lovely. My greatest sexual triumph achieved by proxy.

MILTON: I doubt it was much of a sexual triumph. Remember the demographic I service. Ninety percent of my success is just showing up.

STANLEY: And which of us should show up next time?

MILTON: You want to flip for it?

STANLEY: She isn't going to confuse me for you.

MILTON: Don't be so sure. She already confused —

STANLEY: You for me.

SARAH enters.

SARAH: Have you heard?

MILTON: About Linda?

SARAH: I am getting sacked.

MILTON (*standing*): Would you care to sit?

SARAH: The entire college is being eliminated, and she is getting promoted.

MILTON: She's a dean. Deans get promoted, no matter how wretched they are.

STANLEY: It seems that the only way to get rid of them is to promote them.

MILTON: One of the many perversities of modern economics and management theory.

STANLEY: No doubt the Economics Department will also find a soft landing.

MILTON: Oh yes. Linda was relieved to know that I would be settled in the Business School.

STANLEY (*as if it is an epiphany*): With Helen.

MILTON (*to himself*): Oh heavens. I hadn't considered that.

STANLEY: While Sarah and I are hung out to dry.

MILTON (*to himself*): No, no. This will not do.

SARAH: Yesterday, I thought my work might reshape Western culture. Tomorrow, I'll be looking for a job.

STANLEY: So much for our Greek holiday.

MILTON (*to himself*): I must fix this.

SARAH: Fix what?

MILTON: I can't belong to the same department as the woman I am shagging. It would be worse than living together!

SARAH: I hate men.

MILTON: This is serious.

SARAH: The college is collapsing, and all you can think about is yourself.

MILTON (*with kindness*): Maybe you should spend more time thinking about yourself.

SARAH: What are you talking about?

MILTON: You, Sarah, have your whole life ahead of you. I think that now might be a good time to discuss it.

SARAH: Discuss what?

MILTON: I have business to which I must attend. (*He walks to the door.*) Make her a drink, Stanley, and try to cheer her up. She isn't like us. She is unaccustomed to disappointment and humiliation.

MILTON *exits.*

SARAH (*taking up* MILTON's *chair*): Where is Milton going?

STANLEY: I haven't a clue. But I heard one of our psychology professors say that the best predictor of future behavior is past behavior.

SARAH: So we must imagine —

STANLEY: That he is off to meet some woman.

SARAH: To perform some unspeakable perversion.

STANLEY: Do you care for a drink?

SARAH: I am still feeling poorly from last night.

STANLEY: Aspirin then?

STANLEY *retrieves a bottle of aspirin from a desk drawer and hands it to* SARAH. *While she fumbles with the cap, he pours her a cocktail without missing a beat. He passes it to* SARAH.

SARAH: If I drink this, I may say something that I regret.

STANLEY: You will regret it whether you say it or not.

SARAH: I generally prefer regretting things that I haven't done, rather than regretting things that I have.

STANLEY: Like last night?

SARAH: Yes.

STANLEY: You regret it?

SARAH: Don't you?

STANLEY: Well yes, but I am quite acclimated to uncertainty and regret. Furthermore, I'm not exactly sure what part of the evening I should regret. I have never been blessed with a moral compass — or any compass at all, for that matter.

SARAH (*thinking for a while and sipping her drink*): Maybe you need the right person to give it to you.

STANLEY: Yes, but who would that be? I've always imagined that true purpose must be born from an unlikely source.

There is a knock on the door. Before STANLEY *or* SARAH *can respond,* TRACY *enters full of confidence and dressed to kill.*

TRACY: You wanted to see me, Professor Stevenson?

SARAH (*spinning around in her chair, confrontational*): Tracy.

TRACY (*coldly*): Professor Morgan.

SARAH (*testily*): What brings you here?

TRACY (*equally surly*): I might ask you the same.

SARAH (*done with both of them*): Never mind. It is late. I am going home. I will leave you two to it.

STANLEY: Ah, wait, no, you —

SARAH *stands, takes an aspirin from the bottle, and washes it down by finishing her drink in one gulp. She glares at* TRACY *as she exits.* STANLEY *gathers himself, stands, and motions to* TRACY *to sit.*

STANLEY: Please come in and sit down?

TRACY *sits and crosses her legs in a coquettish manner.*

STANLEY (*sitting as well but flustered*): I am glad you came. I mean, I wanted you…I wanted to…What have you got on your mind?

TRACY (*seductively*): You.

STANLEY: Oh.... Well. (*He stares at her a moment.*) I am going to need a drink. (*He stands and nervously begins making another drink.*) Martini?

TRACY: Yes, please.

> STANLEY *searches for yet another glass, finds one, and starts his drink-making process again.*

STANLEY: How do you take it?

TRACY: However you like.

STANLEY (*to himself*): I am going to regret this.

Scene 6

> STANLEY *is sleeping on the couch in his office, disheveled and snoring. There is a knock on the door. He wakes and slowly gathers himself—straightening his tie, positioning himself in his chair, and kicking his feet up on the desk. There is more knocking.*

STANLEY: Come.

> MILTON *enters. He carries two cups of coffee.*

MILTON: You look satisfied with yourself.

STANLEY: I always am—except when I am woken early in the morning.

MILTON: It stopped being morning hours ago. Have a coffee. (*He sets the coffees on the desk and sits.*) You spent the night here again.

STANLEY: I like the couch.

MILTON: And apparently the company.

STANLEY: Company?

MILTON: I heard that cute coed came by last night.

STANLEY: How is it that everyone knows what happens in my office? It must be bugged.

MILTON: I may have had a hand in Tracy's visiting you.

STANLEY: What did you say to her?

MILTON: The question is not what I said but, rather, what you did.

STANLEY: I didn't do anything.

MILTON: That's two nights in a row.

STANLEY: Two nights?

MILTON: That you slept here, in your office, with company.

STANLEY: Are you worried that the university will start charging me rent?

MILTON: I think the university owes you.

STANLEY: How's that?

MILTON: You haven't heard.

STANLEY: I'm sure I don't know what you are talking about.

MILTON: It's settled.

STANLEY: What's settled?

MILTON: The question of our sexual prowess.

STANLEY spits his coffee.

MILTON: My talents earned you and Sarah the travel grant to Greece, but yours seem to have saved the entire College of Liberal Arts.

STANLEY: You mean —

MILTON: That's right. Whatever you *did* to Tracy worked like a charm. She deleted her incriminating post and replaced it with, well, I hardly know how to describe it.

STANLEY: Please try.

MILTON: She wrote a glorious missive explaining that her Christian values have been strengthened by the liberal arts education she is receiving here.

STANLEY: That's nice.

MILTON: She went on. She said that any person of grace or dignity knows that American values thrive in the cauldron of intellectual discourse and vigorous debate and that she is grateful to the Liberal Arts faculty for challenging and thereby strengthening her love of God and country.

STANLEY: She wrote that?

MILTON: Sarah and Linda suspect that you are the author.

STANLEY: I tell you, man, I am not.

MILTON: Where did she get it?

STANLEY: She is quite capable.

MILTON: Well, her gambit worked like a charm.

STANLEY: The governor backed down?

MILTON: How could he not? Our conservative, Christian governor claimed to be protecting a conservative, Christian coed. He could hardly be her champion if he eliminates the college that she declares is strengthening her faith in God and country.

STANLEY: We may have underestimated the intellectual abilities of our students.

MILTON: And we may have underestimated you.

STANLEY: So Linda and Sarah are off the hook as well?

MILTON: The governor accepted the dean's apology as well as her assurances that the outburst "did not align" with her values and that she is setting aside funding for a safe space for conservative Christians on campus.

STANLEY: Linda wrote that?

MILTON: No, she didn't. I think someone hacked her university account and wrote the message on her behalf.

STANLEY: Well, whoever did it is a genius.

MILTON: I think so, but the real credit goes to you. I guess you chose sex over life.

STANLEY: A gentleman does not kiss and tell.

MILTON: When your romantic talents are so sublime as to rescue the college, I think you are obligated to share them — for academic purposes, of course.

STANLEY: Trust me, my romantic incompetence remains intact.

MILTON: I don't understand. Sarah said that Tracy was like a force of nature — dismissing her with a glance and then advancing on you as a lion advances upon its prey.

STANLEY: I didn't notice. I was staring at her feet.

MILTON: Brilliant.

STANLEY: Contrary to Sarah's characterization, Tracy was practically perfect in every way. I mixed us a few drinks, and we smoked and drank for quite a while. The girl is quite charming.

MILTON: No doubt.

STANLEY: We spoke at length. She spoke of life, of her life, and her studies at the university. She is a liberal arts major, you know.

MILTON: So I've gathered.

STANLEY: She was in a pickle. She did not wish to disappoint her friends in the Christian coalition, nor did she intend to destroy the college and her major with it. So she asked me what I thought she should do.

MILTON: What did you say?

STANLEY: I told her that she would need to decide.

MILTON: That was it?

STANLEY: Yep.

MILTON: You let the fate of the college rest on an existential principle of virtue?

STANLEY: Yep.

MILTON: Like the great Jean-Paul Sartre, you told her that she was condemned to decide on her own, and that even if you gave her advice, she would need to decide whether to take it.

STANLEY: Something like that. But I was drunk, so I was probably slurring my words.

MILTON: You amaze me, Stanley.

STANLEY: What can I say? Beneath this callous exterior, I remain devoted to the Enlightenment.

MILTON: Our task is a simple one: the care and maintenance of civilization.

STANLEY: And having tasted the sweet nectar of civilization, even a hormone-crazed coed like Tracy will succumb to its charms.

MILTON: What did she say?

STANLEY: Nothing really. We talked until dawn. She left, and I fell asleep on the couch.

MILTON: You chose life.

STANLEY: I share this in complete confidence. You must promise not to tell a soul.

MILTON: What about Sarah?

STANLEY: Especially not Sarah. My reputation would be ruined if it ever got out that I didn't take advantage of a willing coed. I would not be able to show my face on this campus again.

MILTON: But Stanley, the situation with Sarah is different.

STANLEY: I know you believe it is, but in this matter, you must trust my instincts. I can only hope that Tracy did not record our conversation. It would reveal my involuntary virtue.

MILTON: Well, it has been quite a day, though you seem to have slept through most of it — along with your classes.

There is a rabid pounding on the door.

MILTON: It seems Tracy has returned for a second attempt.

More pounding.

STANLEY: It is open.

SARAH *enters, rushing in and breathing heavily.*

SARAH: It is over. (*She throws her arms around* STANLEY *and kisses him squarely on the lips. Then turns to* MILTON.) He did it!

MILTON: He is on the front lines of the culture war.

SARAH: He is my hero, our hero. He saved us all.

> SARAH *throws her arms around* MILTON *as well and hugs him unreservedly.*

MILTON: But at what cost to himself?

SARAH: *And* he did it without sleeping with Tracy.

MILTON and STANLEY: What?

SARAH: I know. Even the dean can't believe it.

MILTON: How does the dean know?

SARAH: Because I told her.

MILTON: And how do you know?

STANLEY: My office *is* bugged!

SARAH (*carefully*): Because I left him here yesterday with Tracy at five. At five thirty, he showed up at Helen's house for dinner, their second date in as many days.

> MILTON *spits his coffee.*

STANLEY: It was a busy night…saving the college and securing our travel grant.

MILTON (*recovering*): You are the thin tweed line between civilization and a postmodern chaos.

SARAH: Your romantic dexterity will be legend.

STANLEY: I am a legend all right.

> SARAH's *phone rings. She answers it.*

SARAH: Hello. (*Pause.*) Hi, Linda. (*Pause.*) No, I am in Stanley's office. (*Pause.*) No, I am *not* always in Stanley's office. (*Pause.*) No, I haven't seen it. (*Pause.*) Oh, that is, ah, insane. (*Pause.*) OK. (*She hangs up.*)

MILTON: Our dean?

SARAH: She is on her way here.

MILTON: Why?

SARAH: Apparently, someone hacked the university computer system and posted a bogus ad for the provost position.

MILTON: My heavens.

SARAH: Human Resources has suspended the search.

MILTON: And Linda is no longer the first choice.

SARAH: Not until HR gets to the bottom of this.

STANLEY: Why is she coming here?

SARAH: She thinks you and Milton had something to do with it.

MILTON: Let's go across the street for a drink. Quickly!

MILTON *stands and walks to the door just as* LINDA *enters.*

SARAH: Too late.

LINDA: Which one of you wrote the fake provost ad?

MILTON *and* STANLEY *point at* SARAH.

SARAH: Oh great.

MILTON: It obviously wasn't Stanley. He has been too busy puffing up your résumé by shagging the Arlington Award Scholar.

STANLEY: I haven't slept in days.

LINDA: I plan to have you both fired.

MILTON: If you're to have any chance at the provost spot, when they finally reopen the search, you will need to have Helen Mirandari on your ledger.

SARAH: If she leaves, you are toast.

LINDA: So you are saying —

SARAH: That for the sake of your career, you shouldn't fire Stanley.

LINDA: What about Milton?

STANLEY: Especially not Milton.

LINDA: Why's that?

STANLEY: Because I am shagging the Arlington Award Scholar with his penis.

LINDA and SARAH: What?

MILTON: It's complicated.

LINDA: You two are disgusting.

MILTON: Stanley has —

LINDA: Besmirched the reputation of this college?

MILTON: Saved it.

LINDA turns and exits, storming out.

STANLEY: That's the nicest thing she has said to me in years.

CONSERVATIVE PROTESTERS *shout from offstage:* "Christians have rights, too!" LINDA *responds, offstage as well:* "No, they don't!"

MILTON: Excuse me. I better go and prevent our dean from making a fool of herself again.

CONSERVATIVE PROTESTERS *offstage:* "Christian values are American values!" LINDA *offstage:* "No, they aren't!"

STANLEY: You better hurry.

MILTON *exits.*

SARAH (*sitting next to* STANLEY *and crossing her legs seductively*): So you saved the college and secured our travel grant for Greece. (*She strokes his tweed lapel.*) The thin tweed line.

STANLEY: I really didn't do anything.

SARAH: There is at least one woman on this campus who would beg to differ.

STANLEY: And yet, I have never met her.

SARAH: You don't think you deserve any credit?

STANLEY: I think that the women did all the work.

SARAH: Well, I suppose I owe her thanks for my trip to Greece with you.

STANLEY: Three months in Greece.

SARAH: Are you looking forward to it?

STANLEY: I can think of nothing better.

SARAH: What about your new girlfriend? Aren't you going to miss her?

STANLEY: Which one?

SARAH: How very postmodern of you.

STANLEY: I like to think of my approach to women as an expression of medieval feminism.

SARAH: You're a feminist now?

STANLEY: I think I will call it…"neo-medieval-postmodern-feminism."

SARAH: Catchy. Beyond all socially constructed norms of —

STANLEY: Good and evil.

SARAH: Uh-huh. And your girlfriends approve of your approach?

STANLEY: I don't think they will notice my absence, if that is what concerns you.

SARAH: Good.

STANLEY: You are still l-, l-…

SARAH: A lesbian?

STANLEY: I was going to say "liberated."

SARAH: I am an overworked, underpaid, middle-aged associate professor of philosophy. I am the epitome of liberated.

Curtain

A professor of philosophy, Jack Simmons specializes in metaphysical comedies with romantic twists.

He is the author of *Three Dashes Bitters*, a novel set in the city of New Orleans; the short story "The Painter's Daughter"; and the plays *A Tropical Affair* and *The Thin Tweed Line*.

He is also the editor of *The Twenty-First Century and Its Discontents*, an academic book on contemporary social norms, and coauthor of *Hydrology and Its Discontents*, which examines the intricate web linking water science and society using diverse philosophical lenses.

He was born in California but has spent his adult years in the South. He attended Mandeville High School in Louisiana as well as Louisiana State University and Tulane University.

He lives in Savannah, Georgia, with his wife Katherine and is the proud father of Savannah, Mary, and Augustus.

After classes, he still finds time to sail and enjoy a cocktail (or two) in the evenings.

SwanHorse Press is an imprint of
Monte Ceceri Publishers, LLC

www.ingramcontent.com/pod-product-compliance
Lightning Source LLC
Chambersburg PA
CBHW060535080526
44586CB00012B/738